OUT OF BONDAGE
– Jesus set me free from addiction

Printed by Lightning Source, Milton Keynes, UK

Published by Crossbridge Books
PO Box 848
Worcester
WR6 6SE
Tel: +44 (0)1886 821128

© Crossbridge Books 2011

First published 2011

All rights reserved. No part of this publication may be reproduced, stored in a retrieval system, or transmitted in any form or by any means — electronic, mechanical, photocopying, recording or otherwise — without prior permission of the Publisher.

ISBN 978-0-9561787-8-7

British Library Cataloguing in Publication Data.
A catalogue record for this book is available from the British Library.

Also published by Crossbridge Books:

It's True! Trevor Dearing
The God of Miracles Trevor and Anne Dearing
Schizophrenia Defeated James Stacey
He Has Made Me Glad Glad Rosie
Impossible to Imagine Ruth Parry
COVER by Jonathan Cherry

OUT OF BONDAGE
— Jesus set me free from addiction

ROB GILES
(*The Prodigal Reverend*)

CROSSBRIDGE BOOKS

Dedication

In loving memory of Cousin John, who took his own life on February 4th 1966. This book is dedicated to all who stare the devil in the face and are living on the edge, looking for a way out and finding none. It is dedicated to all alcoholics, drug addicts, anorexics, bulimics, and self harmers and to all who are on the brink of ending it all.

Acknowledgements

I wish to express my gratitude to my wife Maureen, who lived with me and stuck with me through my torment. Many thanks to her for the major part she has played in my journey, in being one of the few sources of stability when everything, within and without, was unstable. I am very grateful for her much love, dedication, commitment and encouragement.

Many thanks to my dear friends who have played an important role in my journey: To Alan Southall, John Catchpole, Martyn Parkes, Francis De Silva, Mary Noott, Jill Berry, Steve Buck, David Edwards, Peter Lane and Brian Rose. Without their friendship I would have gone under.

Special thanks must be given to Wilf Harding who not only played an important role in my journey but helped me get started in the initial stages of writing, and scrutinised the script in the later stages. Special thanks must also be given to David Johnson, for his help and the very many hours of checking and re-checking the manuscript. It feels as though I have undergone a massive lesson in the English language because of these two gentlemen.

I would also like to thank the Reverend George Miller who encouraged me to write my story down. I am very grateful for his support and enthusiasm in writing the foreword.

I extend my gratitude to all those who have read through the manuscript and have given me their much valued feedback.

I acknowledge all who played a part in my journey, both for good and for bad. To all who caused me harm, wittingly or unwittingly; there is no animosity on my part. Without your part the story would not be complete and I would not be the person I am today.

Finally, I acknowledge and extend my gratitude and thanks to my Saviour, Jesus Christ, who stepped into the self-destructive chaos of my life and of my mind and turned things completely around. Without which I would still be a lost soul, trapped in an endless cycle of bad choices, destined for ruin and having no message of hope.

Contents

	Page
Foreword by George Miller	xi
Introductory Chapter	1

The Downward Spiral and the Upward Turn

Chapter 2..... Unfulfilled Dreams	6
Chapter 3..... On the Dung-hill	15
Chapter 4..... New Beginnings	26
Chapter 5..... Steps to Recovery	33

The Revelatory Visions that Changed My Thinking

Chapter 6..... Two Gems	40
Chapter 7..... A Change of Heart ... A Change of Mind	50
Chapter 8..... Repentance (in a way I'd never seen before	59
Chapter 9..... Trust and Obey	69

The Prayer that Changed My Life

Chapter 10..... The Prayer of Quiet	78
Chapter 11..... The Secret Place	89
Chapter 12..... The Turnaround Prayer	99

Facing the Truth

Chapter 13..... Back to the Start (a Way for God's Direction) 108

Chapter 14..... The Mantles 118

Chapter 15..... A Bizarre Encounter 128

Chapter 16..... Choices, Growth and Breakthrough 136

Summing Up

Chapter 17..... Roots 147

Chapter 18..... Putting Things into Perspective 161

Bibliography & Suggested Books for Further Reading 170

BIBLICAL QUOTATIONS
Scripture quotations are taken from the New King James Version of the Bible unless otherwise stated.

Foreword

I have known Rob Giles for many years; we have ministered together many times in the past. However, we had not seen each other in years. When we met up recently I had to look twice before I was convinced it was the same Rob. I am sure he felt the same about me.

As we sat together in our Board Room and Rob began to tell me his story I listened to his painfully real and honest journey from bondage to freedom in Christ. It was a story many others needed to hear, I encouraged Rob to write his story.

As I read the manuscript I saw the awfulness and torment of satanic bondage, drugs, alcohol and pornography; but even more important was the way to freedom. If a man of Rob's standing can become so enslaved then we need to be on our guard. Don't be so pious saying, "it could never happen to me". Scripture says: "Let him that thinks He stands take heed lest he fall".

Rob shares honestly and openly his real struggles, and as you read you will become aware of the reality of spiritual warfare... "We do not wrestle against flesh and blood but against principalities, against powers, against the rulers of the darkness of this age, against spiritual hosts of wickedness in the heavenly places".

These forces are real but there really is freedom; you will discover how prayer and revelation from God help to bring freedom. Whether or not you are in bondage, this book will be a blessing to you and could help you to help others — a very good read.

Rob, thanks again for your honesty — this book will be a blessing to hundreds.

George Miller. November 2010.

George was formerly a Pastor within the Elim Pentecostal group of Churches. Later he became an international Evangelist and founder of Reconciliation Ministries International. He has worked extensively in the U.K. and the Caribbean.

Introductory Chapter

> See a young man fettered
> Shackled and bound in chains
> Deeply cut with sorrow
> And pierced with addiction pains
> As he quietly prayed and prayed
> The smaller he became
> Smaller, still smaller in his own eyes
> Until he slipped those chains
>
> *Rob Giles 2010*

Out of Bondage! What kind of title is that? Bondage is not a pleasant word, nor is it one that people would normally choose to associate themselves with. I'm not talking in this instance of a person who is literally bound with ropes or chains, neither am I thinking of the sexually deviant practice called by the same name. What I mean by the term is anything a person becomes dependent on or addicted to and cannot break free.

A person who is contending for freedom, wrestling with an addiction or dependency, would rarely use the term 'bondage' to describe their condition. However, when they are through to the other side, and they look back, they may well say out loud as I did, "My, oh my, **that** was indeed bondage!!.... I was nothing less than a **slave**!!" That is precisely how I feel about it. It was a horrid time and a horrid place to be. I never want to

CHAPTER ONE

go back to it (with God's help).

We live in an age where the mere pressures of everyday living are phenomenal. Stress and anxiety take their toll upon us to an alarming extent. It is most unfortunate that in an attempt to escape or find a moment's comfort from the stresses of life, many will turn to alcohol. It is socially acceptable to have a drink or two, and it is well known that alcohol, in moderation, is a mild de-stressing agent. Tragically, there are those who take too much. Some will end up in a far deeper pit than the one they're already in. They will become binge drinkers or alcoholics; enslaved, and in bondage to drink, drugs or whatever the chosen substance. As a result, they may also lose their livelihood, their home, their marriage, their family and end up on the streets. Such is the destructive power of alcohol abuse.

This is the story of my journey as a **Christian**. I have highlighted the word Christian because the depth to which I spiralled out of control is not the place for a Christian to be. I sank into the depth of despair as a result of stress and anxiety. I journeyed through alcoholism and mental and emotional trauma which led to a breakdown. I also fell into the additional anguish of sexual fantasy and pornography, all of which held me firmly in their grip... to the point where, together with the drink, they very nearly destroyed my mind, my marriage and my life. I came to the place where I wanted to die — a chilling fact — but for the grace of God.

I am very conscious, however, that I have but sipped from the **poisoned chalice** of alcoholism, and mental and emotional trauma. Others of you out there may have drunk more deeply from that bitter cup. Be that as it may, my experience was real, painful and very traumatic.

I used the unusual method of **prayer** with which to break free. This narrative then is an account of the work of God in to find themselves in a similar mess to my own (or worse). It is written for those who journey through the quagmire of such pains and for those who stare the devil in the face or looking down the barrel of a loaded gun. When a person has genuinely come through alcoholism, it really does feel as though one has stared the devil in the face. When you have come within an inch of your life, so to speak, it is as though you have looked down the barrel of a loaded gun. Ask any alcoholic in recovery, and they will tell you the same!

This book is written for those who cannot find the freedom they crave by ordinary means, and it is written for those who seek Spiritual answers to their queries. Most of all I have written it to encourage everyone not to give up, for there is a way out!

It is my pleasure, therefore, to declare that there is freedom to be found in the person of Jesus Christ. Not only so, but there is also mental, emotional and physical healing to be grasped in Him. To discover that there is a possible way out, when all else has failed, is very precious and priceless beyond description. So I commend this, my story, to you.

I urge you therefore, dear friend, and appeal to you as one 'beggar' to another, to join me and walk with me on this my journey of discovery. So take my hand... let us walk together...

The Downward Spiral and the Upward Turn

2

Unfulfilled Dreams

> You dream of this, you dream of that
> To live the dream I hear you say
> Will it make you happy? Will it make you sad?
> When the dream's fulfilled on that glorious day
> But wait! Not always does it work like this;
> Nor does it work like that
> For no one great or small can know
> What grief may come their way.
> *Rob Giles 2010*

It was during the winter of 1994 that I made my first trip to Croatia with a charity, based in Bromsgrove, to take aid to refugee camps there. The war between Serbia and Croatia was just about over. However, Serbia was still at war with Bosnia and many Bosnian refugees poured over the border into Croatia seeking sanctuary. The Croatian government and the United Nations set up many refugee camps; it was to some of these that we took the aid.

We left the shores of the U.K. about a week before Christmas, taking the ferry from Dover to Dunkirk. It was a convoy of three trucks and a minibus with a trailer. I was in the minibus. I'd taken my guitar along, with the intention of playing a few songs in some of the camps.

Suddenly one of our team exclaimed, "Hey look! There's a trailer overtaking us!" Somehow on our journey through Belgium along the A3 the trailer had become detached from the minibus. I glanced through the window to see it running alongside us, giving the impression that it was trying to overtake the bus. The trailer hit the crash barrier, somersaulted and smashed in pieces, spilling its precious cargo over the hard shoulder.

Just prior to impact there was a bizarre moment. A vehicle was joining the motorway from the right and for a split second, the minibus, the trailer and the car were all in line as though racing towards the chequered flag. The car managed to squeeze in between the crash barrier and the trailer just in time to avoid the collision. I dread to think what might have been.

Never have I seen police arrive at a scene so quickly. It was as if by magic they appeared out of nowhere within moments (at least that's how it seemed). Needless to say we had to leave the trailer in a service area and go on without it. We salvaged what we could of our consignment and shared it amongst the trucks and the minibus, and then continued on our journey.

Our first stop was a motel in Leuven, about 20 km the other side of Brussels. The philosophy of the aid agency we were with was to ensure volunteers get a good night's sleep. The trip as a whole would be hard work and taxing enough without making it more difficult by sleeping in the cab. So it was that we had a very nice meal and a cosy bed for the night in the said motel.

Next day we travelled across Germany heading out towards the Austrian border. A beautiful place called Adlersburg near Regensburg was where we spent our second night. Adlersburg

CHAPTER TWO

gave its name to a vast estate of great natural beauty and to the home of its proprietor. The buildings, the rooms, the service and the food set it apart from the average. Herr Adler, a gentleman in his late seventies and the proprietor of the establishment, happened to be there that night. We had our evening meal and were sitting at the table chatting and finishing off our drinks, when he came over to us having discovered that we were English.

From that moment on the drinks were on him. In the course of our conversation, we learned that he had travelled the world hunting, and then he began to tell us stories of his adventures. One by one everyone in our party took their leave and slipped away to their beds leaving Mike, one of the team members, and myself alone with Herr Adler.

We were drinking Black Beer followed by Schnapps chasers way into the early hours of the morning. The staff had long since put the chairs on the tables, turned out the lights and gone home. Mike and I followed Herr Adler into his kitchen where he produced a bottle of Russian Vodka out of one of his many fridges. This bottle allegedly had been brought back from the Russian front during the Second World War. He said that it had been kept for a special occasion and we appeared to be that special occasion. "Very nice too!" So I thought. It didn't take long to empty the bottle between the three of us. A couple of hours later we were ready to resume our journey and I was throwing up on Herr Adler's car park.

You see, I had a drink problem. However, I was totally unaware of it and I certainly would not have admitted it to anyone at that time in my life. When I became a Christian in the summer of 1971, I walked away from alcohol completely and should really have stayed that way. It was about fifteen years later that I took a drink at a wedding, having been convinced that it was 'O.K' for a Christian to have a drink.

That drink at the wedding proved to be disastrous for me.

We travelled through Austria and Slovenia to a hotel in Croatia; this was to be our base for the next few days. We visited an orphanage, a school and various camps; the whole thing was very moving. I recall being moved with compassion as I stood and played a short concert in a camp on the border of Bosnia. They were hungry for more than food. When I had finished, Tony the leader of our group came out dressed as Santa Claus and gave out presents to everyone there. One old lady broke down and cried. She hadn't seen Santa Claus for 40 years.

I made five trips in total and I loved it. This was a good time for me because I had the feeling I was achieving something. I was unperturbed by some of the scenes we witnessed and I wasn't bothered about the strange food either, as some of our party were. I found that I could easily adapt to each and every situation as it arose, from seeing appalling conditions in a camp on the border of Bosnia to being held up at a border crossing for a long period of time or on a return journey being stopped by the German police. For me it was all part of the trip and part of the adventure. I began to feel for the first time I was doing something worthwhile.

All the time I was trying to press towards 'full time ministry' in a vain attempt to 'fulfil my dream'. I went to the Midlands Bible College (Wolverhampton) part-time in 1996 to study for a Diploma in Pastoral Ministry along with a Cambridge Certificate in Religious Studies. I subsequently graduated in 1998, being one of only two students to be ordained that year. My application for ordination was accepted on the grounds of my missions work and aid relief trips to the refugee camps in Croatia. I was ordained as a missionary.

Shortly after graduation, I became the interim pastor of a

CHAPTER TWO

small Pentecostal church. Every step of the way I had prayed fervently, read my Bible seeking guidance from God. Verses of Scripture stood out to me, the majority of which related to the Good Shepherd. This was foremost in my mind as I took up this temporary post. The little Church was made up of mainly elderly people who paid me something towards my travel expenses as they couldn't afford to pay me full-time. I kept my full-time job to support the family whilst looking after the Church part-time.

The mandate that I felt from God was simply to love and care for them. Yes! I did have a mandate from God. I'd sought it fervently through prayer during the weeks prior to taking up my post and I tried to fulfil it with all of my heart. I was sent there as a Shepherd. It seemed to me to be a great honour and a privilege to serve them. "Just go there and love them," was the message I felt God was saying to my heart. It was a great encouragement to me that they enjoyed my preaching and Bible teaching. I enjoyed it too, delving around in the scriptures and bringing out little gems that sometimes astounded me. Devotional preaching on Sunday morning, Gospel preaching in the evening, Bible study Tuesday night; I was in my element and loved it. 'Could this be the ministry I longed for?' I asked myself.

It was a forty mile round trip to the church and I was grateful for what they paid me, for it took the strain off our finances during that season. Three couples very kindly offered to take it in turns to invite me to Sunday lunch; this enabled me to cut down on the travelling and also gave me much needed opportunities to get to know the members of the Church. In between lunch and tea I seized the opportunity for pastoral visitation.

I wasn't there long before I was faced with my first major challenge; a funeral. I had taken many funerals in the past but this was different. The funeral was that of a young man, the son of one of our church members who was of Caribbean origin. Tragically, he had hanged himself. I'd never officiated at a funeral where the deceased had taken his own life and neither had I ever attended so large a funeral gathering.

The church was packed like sardines in a can. People were standing in the aisles and at the back of the building; they filled the doorway and were crammed in the porch. I discovered at the end of the service that there was a large group assembled out on the car park listening to the service.

I was unfazed by it all and took it in my stride. As I stood on the platform, the coffin was duly opened true to Caribbean custom and everyone began filing by the casket, one by one, to pay their last respects.

As everyone filed past the coffin, I thought to myself, 'What a great opportunity.' I glanced around at the congregation and compassion seized me at that moment. I said nothing about suicide; I just performed a straightforward funeral service and in a short address, I preached the Gospel declaring simply that Jesus is longing to step into our lives and to share our grief. "Come to me all of you who are weary and heavy-laden and I will give you rest" was the verse of Scripture and as lovingly and as inoffensively as I could, I presented Christ to them. I trod very carefully, being aware that one could all too easily say the wrong thing, given the sensitive nature of that particular funeral.

Later I thought to myself, 'I've arrived! I'm now living my dream.' This truly was where I had longed to be ever since I first became a Christian in the July of 1971 and these were the very people I had dreamt of reaching with the love of God. Oh how I prayed that it would not end!!

At the graveside after the committal, one by one the male

CHAPTER TWO

relatives and friends, beginning with the father and ending with acquaintances, took a shovel to fill in the grave. "I love Caribbean funerals," joked one of the cemetery's gravediggers, as I stepped out of the way, "I don't have to fill in the graves." I smiled and we chatted together for about twenty minutes until our Caribbean brethren had completed the task. When a person from the West Indies says, "We bury our dead", they mean it, literally!

Pastoring that little Church was for me a most marvellous experience; my only disappointment was that Maureen my wife was not with me in the venture. I had to serve largely alone. Serving alone was not in itself a problem but something was missing: the mere fact that my wife was not there. Maureen was involved in our parent Church and needed to be at home for our family. I had easy access to the Superintendent Minister of the West Midlands Pentecostal Churches for support. Jill Berry, the Minister of our parent Church, had also agreed to support and offer advice if I needed it.

The Church wanted me to stay on and become their permanent pastor, which truthfully I'd have loved to do. The Superintendent Minister was happy to go along with whatever the Church wanted. I, on the other hand, had taken on the post initially for six months and was working towards handing over to someone else. I had agreed to stay for a further three months whilst the Superintendent Minister continued the search for a permanent replacement. I was being advised by Maureen and Jill as to the difficulties that might ensue if I were to take up the post on a permanent basis. Jill put forward the name of a gentleman who was currently available and looking for the next stage of his ministry. I had heard him preach in the past and had been very impressed by his message. I agreed (reluctantly) that he was right for the job. I think if I'm honest I wanted to stay.

Subsequently there were interviews. He was booked to preach in order that the Church as a whole could get the 'feel of the guy', as we put it, when we are checking someone out. After all was said and done, it was up to the members; they had the final say regarding who should be their pastor. Finally, all parties involved agreed and so we proceeded to work together towards his inauguration as the new pastor.

He did have an inspired vision for the Church and I was surprised when he asked me to stay on and help. He wanted to lead the Church and for me to do the pastoral work. He believed that I possessed qualities he lacked. I was flattered but after thinking matters over I concluded that it wouldn't work for me. I thought that at some point we would surely clash.

He had a very strong personality and was a very driven sort of person. If I stayed true to God's directive, I would have had to stand up for the flock and fight their corner if he tried to 'railroad' changes through. However, as I am the kind of person who does not relish confrontation, I feared there would be difficulties. I would be placing myself in a compromising situation. I figured it would be better for him if I were not there.

Undoubtedly, it would have been a different ball game if Maureen was there with me and we were in it together; it might very well have worked then. So, I declined his invitation, thanked him for his very kind offer and moved on to what I thought would be the next phase of **my** ministry. I had no idea that would not be the case.

I was there twelve months in total. Oh, how I wished I could have stayed on! And the Church too had pleaded with me to stay. However, a permanent move would have put a tremendous strain on our marriage, with the two of us not working together. Having to make decisions on my own; all the travelling; living separate lives; maybe we would have drifted apart. I consoled myself with this reasoning.

I reluctantly worked with all parties to see the new pastor installed. Secretly, however, I was devastated. I was unaware of the connection at the time, but it was then I began turning to alcohol much, much more. I actually went downhill very rapidly after that.

3

On the dung-hill

>Slipping down, sinking down
>How far will you go?
>Where you lose your dignity
>Will you really know?
>For Job it was the dung-hill
>And Christ became a 'worm'
>How far must you fall, dear soul?
>Before you start to squirm...
>
>*Rob Giles 2010*

I was in a pressure job in the aviation industry, making parts for aircraft when I left that small Church. The workplace itself was no different from any other engineering factory. It was the level of precision and accuracy, and the high level of responsibility and accountability that set it apart from mainstream engineering. Every part made was traceable to the persons who made it. That person was responsible. If a part failed in an aircraft and it was discovered in the subsequent inquiry that it was down to the negligence of those who made the part, then they were held accountable.

The pressure was getting to me. I was rapidly sinking and beginning to fall apart. I hated the aggression of the management, and I hated my job. I drank to relieve the

CHAPTER THREE

pressure and due to the fact that alcohol was so cheap to buy at an off-licence or supermarket, I would drink at home rather than go out.

To put it in my own words, "I didn't drink any old booze just to get a fix". I only drank what I considered to be the best, such as Premium lagers, South African or Australian red wines and Scotch. And if I could afford it, I'd indulge in a 'wee dram' of the finest malt whisky ('wee dram' being a whole bottle!). My drinking took the form of bingeing and almost every night became a mini-binge.

Once, at a party, I drank myself senseless. There was a marquee outside and the drinks were free. I can remember drinking four or five Southern Comforts and several beers, but after that I have no recollection of what I drank. I passed out in the garden and came round the next morning soaked to the skin; someone had thrown a bucket of water over me. Later I discovered it was to wash away the vomit.

My ribs ached as if I'd been kicked. I imagined that the host was so disgusted with me that he'd given me the kicking I deserved. In actual fact it turned out that I was lying on my back vomiting and a fellow lifted me up and gave me a bear hug to make sure that I brought everything up before putting me in the recovery position. That's where I was when I came round — in the recovery position. That gentleman may very well have saved my life.

Maureen said to me when I got home: "You've got a drink problem. You can't drink like a normal person."

"Don't talk wet," I replied, "I'm in control; I know what I'm doing; I can take it or leave it."

Famous last words. My wife was right, I did have a problem and I really couldn't drink like a responsible person — I didn't sip or drink slowly but often downed the stuff in one. If I opened a bottle I had to finish it off, I could not leave it; to put the cork back in the bottle was sacrilege to me and a waste. But I couldn't see it. I was in denial.

I'll never forget the first time I became aware that I really did have a drink problem. The occasion was the wedding of a family member. It was a beautiful wedding and everyone had a good time and I got "well oiled", as we say where I come from. Several weeks later, a copy of the wedding video was passed around the family.

I recall sitting and watching the video with Maureen, her brother Phil and his wife Lynn, at our home. We were laughing and enjoying reliving the moments together. Then Phil said, "Watch this!" There was a clip of me. I was appalled at my behaviour. Then there was another clip of me and someone joked, "Hey! Here comes the phantom groper again." I felt sickened; it was then I thought to myself, "Rob, old son, you've got a drink problem."

Before that moment it was just boozing, binge drinking and being sick occasionally, but that moment watching the wedding video was when I first became aware of my alcoholism. That was when my troubles really started, because I soon discovered that it wasn't at all easy to give it up. I couldn't stop drinking just like that. People said to me things like: "You've got the power to say no," and: "Every day we all make choices; you can choose". But it wasn't that simple; it just doesn't work like that when you're addicted, and that goes for any kind of addiction, not just drink and drugs. "That's a cop-out!" folk would say to me, "You're just making excuses," or "You don't really want to give it up. If you wanted to give it up you could do it." I don't have a strong argument in reply to their apparently sound reasoning. All I know is this: it just doesn't work like that. It is almost as if one's choice has been taken away. You really have to be there to know what it's like. This

CHAPTER THREE

is the paradox of addiction.

For me however, it was no longer just simply drinking; I was now aware that I was addicted to the 'jolly stuff' and I could not get free. It is true that when you realise you've a problem, that's when your troubles begin. It is also true that when you realise you have a problem it is the first step to recovery.

There was a great aching in my heart. I disliked what I was becoming but I did not have the power, the ability or the strength to change; and believe me, I really did try. I became depressed; I had no ministry; my job was soul-destroying and I also disliked the behaviour of the people I worked with. I was stressed to the hilt and the anxiety was beginning to cripple me — 'cripple' is an apt description because I was greatly restricted and limping emotionally. On top of all that, I was now aware that I was addicted to alcohol.

I was fast becoming unable to think or act in a rational fashion. My mind was also turning more and more to fantasies, which I was very soon unable to control.

As a child I often withdrew into a fantasy world; it was for me a way of comfort and a way of escape. During the school year of 1962-63 I wrote a play. I approached the English teacher and asked her if she thought it was worthy enough for members of my form to produce it for the school. She read it and agreed to my request.

It was a huge success and the school was buzzing. For weeks afterwards pupils were talking about the performance. This fool wrote it, produced it, directed it and played a small part in it and I never got any credit for it at all. There wasn't any encouragement from the teacher and no attempt was made to nurture or to foster the potential I may or may not have possessed. I remember feeling bemused by the teacher's response. I said to myself things like, 'Why did she do that?'

and, 'Was it because I'm the most unlikely student to write it?' And then I thought to myself, 'Maybe it's because I'm not the teacher's pet.' I really didn't expect the teacher to give the credits to others and then announce it publicly to the whole school.

But hey! I could withdraw into my fantasy world and be whatever I wanted to be. I could be the 'hero'. I could be a George Bernard Shaw, another Hitchcock or Errol Flynn. There in my fantasies I could be anything and do anything and certainly no one could ever hurt me there (so I thought).

I withdrew to the realm of fantasy from time to time as an adult, but it was now beginning to get beyond my control. The realm of fantasy can be a very dangerous place to be, simply because it is unreality and as such it is a lie and not truth. For me, however, there was a further, more sinister danger; the fantasies were turning into visions. The fantasies had become more and more sexual in nature, and as they were developing into visionary scenes before my eyes and in my mind, the dangers I'm sure are evident.

There was a terrifying moment when a dream was invaded. I say 'invaded' because the dream was in no way self-induced. I say 'terrifying' because it was a moment when the dream touched reality. I awoke in a sweat, my heart beating at a terrific rate, scared witless; all of my senses were alive with the scene at the moment of waking. Never before in my entire life had I recalled smells and tastes from a dream. But this was the moment where the dream and reality merged. For several hours after waking the smell and the taste lingered. It seemed to me as if the final image was being burned indelibly on my mind. I tremble, even now, as I think of that awful encroachment, and the demonic violation of my mind and senses.

That was bad enough but foolishly I fed it. Pornography was readily available in the workplace. This added further fuel

CHAPTER THREE

to the fire that was already raging inside me and only served to compound my problems and add to my depression. Drink, fantasy and pornography were a lethal cocktail and all three became a devilish addiction.

Together these three were slowly destroying my mind. It was at this point that there were voices in my head narrating the visions and fantasies and giving a running commentary, making my whole being come alive to that fantasy. My body and my senses appeared alive — so much so that I was fast becoming unable to discern the difference between fantasy and reality. This was the danger point.

I couldn't tell Maureen about my plight because I was far too ashamed. She must have known something was going on beyond that which she could see, even if she didn't know exactly what. She's certainly no fool.

During that period of time I must have been a nightmare to live with. At the slightest thing I would fly into a rage. I was becoming a very angry man. I was angry at every mortal thing that went wrong and in my emotionally unstable state I'd swear and throw things around or kick something up in the air. The pressure inside me was like a shaken bottle of fizzy pop ready to explode. I was puffing and blowing constantly to relieve the pressure, which is terribly infuriating to those around. Everything was against me and slipping away from my grasp and I couldn't stop it.

I was up and down like a yo-yo, so to speak. The highs and the lows were poles apart and there was very little of anything that resembled calmness and stability in between. When I was high, people would often say to me, "Are you on drugs or something?" or, "Could you give me some of what you're on?"

For the most part, however, I was down and depressed. Paranoia, fear and anxiety intensified. Everything inside me was like an elastic band stretched to the limit and ready to break, and yet in the midst of it all I could still get higher than a kite. Mentally I was breaking down; I could no longer think rationally; and decision making was almost impossible, which threw me into a blind panic and a fierce rage.

Maureen and I had rows, verbally violent rows, and in the end my favourite line and get-out clause was, "You don't understand what's happening to me." I accused her of not understanding, but I couldn't understand either what was happening to me.

She was afraid to tell me things, not knowing how I would react. She said more than once, "I can't tell you anything any more; you're out of control; you frighten me." I **was** out of control. Completely out of control, pressing the self-destruct button and heading for a breakdown.

I rapidly reached the stage where I was a physical and emotional wreck and could no longer work, displaying symptoms of chronic fatigue syndrome. My doctor gave me a sick note. I can't remember what he'd written on that note but I knew I had broken down mentally and emotionally.

I left the pornography at that time but it didn't leave me. The pornography was in my head, in the fantasies and in the visions. The visions were awful; they were nightmares — or should I say 'day-mares', like a pornographic movie playing in my head with a running commentary. I could not switch it off, demonic stuff that I couldn't describe, nor would I wish to.

The fantasies and the visions became of longer duration. I could be locked into either for several days at a time and could involuntarily or voluntarily revisit a fantasy vision. I was torn as I fluctuated between enjoying and hating those fantasies. Yes! I did say 'enjoying'. I wouldn't be telling the truth if I were to say there wasn't enjoyment in the participation. It was after the event that the hatred came; hatred of the visions and

CHAPTER THREE

demonic oppression, yes, but mainly self-hatred and self-loathing. I most certainly would not have admitted any of these things to anyone at that time. I was, however, on a journey of self-discovery; not a very pleasant journey but again crucial to recovery.

Alcohol only served to make matters worse. I longed to stop drinking, longed to switch off the fantasies and the visions in my head. "Where are you God?" I often cried out. "There has to be a way out," I prayed and reasoned with myself. "There must be a way out." To put it politely and biblically, I was now sitting on a 'dung-hill'. Drug addicts and alcoholics who are rock-bottom call it something less dignified.

I feared I was swiftly moving to the edge of insanity. I was very conscious of what was happening to me, so I played things down with my doctor. I didn't want to be put away. I also convinced him enough not to give me medication. I did agree, however, to have counselling and went along for a couple of sessions at the surgery. I longed to be able to talk with the counsellor about the pornographic visions and the torment I was in. I longed to speak about my addiction to the drink. But alas, the counsellor was female and young enough to be my daughter. I bottled out with shame and bluffed my way through the sessions. I hated what I'd become. I felt so alone, so completely alone.

Throughout all of this I never stopped going to church. If there was to be a breakthrough, or if I was to break this cycle, I reasoned: 'Surely it would be here in church!' 'There has to be a way out,' I kept telling myself. I went forward in meetings looking for and expecting a miracle.

I sought Christian counselling. This proved difficult. Of course I needed someone I could really trust, but the real problem lay within me. SHAME! Shame was like a curse, crippling me, holding me back; holding me fast in bondage. 'Is there any way out?' I questioned.

I had got rid of everything that I thought might be offensive and repented over and over again; but nothing changed on the inside. I had often heard the message in church: "All you have to do is repent and ask God for forgiveness and He'll change you." Why was this not working? I was asking for forgiveness constantly. Every action and every thought that was remotely evil I repented of. I went through all of the formulae for deliverance that the Church teaches.

Avidly I read the Bible, particularly the words of Jesus, looking for any morsel that came from His lips that would reveal to me the way out. What had He got to say about the mess I was in? What was I doing wrong? Why could I not get free? Where was the victory that Christ won? These were the questions I asked myself and asked in prayer over and over again. It felt as if Christ had died in vain. I was heart-broken and rock-bottom.

I was off work for about three months and then started back to work two or three days a week under the direction of the doctor. It was Hell. The torment in my mind, the fire in my breast, and devilish visions suggested to me that this was indeed the closest to Hell I'd ever get on earth.

There was at this point a feeling as if a steel belt was tightening around my chest. The pain was intense and the anxiety crippling. There was a feeling like something bleeding into my soul, poisoning me; this is the only way I can describe it. I wept rivers of tears. I cried to God for help and to take away the pain. It was debilitating and there was no let-up. It was constant as though my very life was draining away. It did actually feel as though I was slowly dying. I felt desperately ill and I wanted to die but I couldn't — I was held back. Often this was my prayer: "Lord take my life, I don't want to live any

CHAPTER THREE

longer." The visions and the nightmares were horrifying but they were nothing in comparison to this **pain**. I believe this is what's called a broken heart — and there seemed no way out.

I was under pressure from the management to resume full-time employment and to operate the machine I formerly worked on. I was in fact following my doctor's orders by working two or three days per week and doing menial tasks whilst recovering. The management were very intimidating and manipulative in the pressure they were exerting.

During this time I was seeing Francis, an old friend who was a Christian. He was very helpful, being prepared to listen empathically to some of my story. He didn't judge me or criticise me at all; he listened and committed me to God. This was very important to me because I felt scared to share my woes with anyone lest they rejected me. I thought that if the Church leaders discovered the mess I was in they'd put me out of the Church. I was at times thinking that even Jesus Christ himself had cast me out.

One piece of advice my friend gave was to write down the things that took place at work and maybe talk to someone at Citizens' Advice Bureau. I began to catalogue the intimidating, manipulative and implied threats. I recorded events and things as they happened, and went along to the C.A.B. I found that I did have a potential case against my employers.

Then the day came when I was pressured (intimidated and threatened indirectly) into returning to the lathe, the machine that I formerly operated. I was struck with terror and had the shakes and tremors inside so badly I couldn't think properly to do the job. I said, "I can't do this, I've got the shakes; it's too soon, much too soon." I was given an implied ultimatum which amounted to: "Either work that machine or leave." They were very careful not to make it a direct threat. But I knew what they meant.

I no longer had any fight left in me. I had neither the physical, mental or emotional capacity to take the matter any further. So I capitulated and walked away. I was floundering. I now had no job and I was unable to sign on for unemployment benefit because I'd walked out of my own accord. I felt at that moment as though I'd lost everything. Everything, that is, except my family; I was spared that horror.

4

New Beginnings

> When you're broken and disgraced —
> God has not forgotten
> Should you fall flat on your face
> Or if you sink rock-bottom
> God is at work behind the scenes.
> When you're just not winning
> He longs to lovingly restore
> And give a new beginning.
>
> Rob Giles 2010

When I walked out of that place it felt as though a great weight had been lifted from my shoulders; that was in the September of 2002. Day by day that hellish pain or ache in my chest and the bleeding poison that was seeping into my soul and slowly sucking the life out of me began to subside. It did take several months, but oh what a glorious feeling! It was like being in heaven. I couldn't stop giving thanks and praise to God the day that it left me. I was so relieved to be free of that horrid pain.

I managed to get a temporary job within a few days of my 'walkout'. Ironically it was in engineering, operating the same machine on which I had the breakdown. I held on to that job for a couple of months before I was released. It wasn't easy holding on to it, but I did it long enough to acquire sufficient money to see us as a family through the Christmas period. Because I wasn't sacked I could now at least sign on and get unemployment benefit.

What happened next was surreal. Well, at least, that is how it felt. There were no changes to the mess I was in with regard to the drink and visions except I was being healed of that horrid pain. Yet at the same time I was being carried along, being borne aloft towards being self-employed. If a person is going through an emotional and mental breakdown, it really isn't a good time to start a business. I was very conscious of that, but it was happening; it was unfolding before me. Something other than me; something outside of me was putting everything into place, shielding me from the pressure and consequential stress and bearing me aloft. That is the only way I can think to describe what was taking place.

It was in the February of 2003 that I took my first job working for myself. I was allowed to work up to 16 hours per week and still sign on. Maureen and I were hoping to continue with the 16hrs a week for about six weeks and officially start at the beginning of April. A new tax year seemed to be a good time to launch the new venture. This we agreed with the DHSS. However, due to a clerical error on my part I was automatically signed off.

"What are we to do now?" I said to my wife, trembling and holding the letter from the DHSS in my hand.

"Let's go for it," she replied.

So we did.

We registered the business with the Inland Revenue, met with an accountant and started up on March 17th 2003. We had to buy many tools but we chose not to go into debt. It was a drain on our resources but we managed. My biggest concern

CHAPTER FOUR

was: "Where will we get the work from?"

Maureen said, "Let's trust the Lord."

I shudder now when I think about it. Normally I would have folded in a situation such as this. The fear and anxiety would have got the better of me and to put it colloquially, I would have thrown my teddy out of the pram and gone into a blind panic. Yet I was somehow shielded from that kind of pressure. It was surreal: I was being sustained.

One of the most important things to me at that time was that my wife supported the venture. We were in this together and that was terrific. We were advised by the accountant to start up as a partnership rather than that of a Sole Trader. So Maureen became my business partner; I did the manual work and she kept the books.

I was trading as a carpenter. I loved hanging doors and found it to be therapeutic. Fitting doors turned out to be the main thrust of our business, the majority of which I did for the public. I didn't particularly like site work; it felt too similar to working in a factory. As the business built up I was able to be more selective in the type of work that I took on, so I quit the site work. Being in a position where you can choose the work you do is one of the many plus factors of being self-employed.

I enjoyed going into people's homes, having a friendly chat and a cup of tea and seeing that glorious look of approval in their eyes when the job was done. I had been starved of this in industry. I'd go home tired but with a satisfied mind, knowing that I'd worked hard and done a good job. What a privileged position I was now in! I was now doing a job I really loved. It truly was medicine to me.

I no longer had the physical strength I once possessed but that didn't matter. I was finding enough strength from God for each day. Whether I had a heavy workload or a very light schedule, I had enough strength to see it through. From Day

One of starting up I was conscious that the business was God's business. I certainly could not have done this on my own. God was at work here. These were my genuine thoughts at that time.

During the summer of 2004 a friend and I had been trying to get together for a walk. We had made several attempts at making arrangements and had failed. Something unexpected always seemed to turn up to scupper our plans and we re-scheduled over and over again. Martyn had two boys with whom he spent much of his time, particularly during the summer months, so we finally figured it would make better sense if we did our walk after they were back at school. We fixed a mutually acceptable time in September with the intention of walking part of the North Worcestershire Path.

This is a path for walkers that winds its way for thirty miles from Kingsford Country Park near Kinver, across north Worcestershire over the Clent Hills, Waseley Beacon, the Lickey Hills and Forhill to finish at Major's Green near Shirley. We chose to walk a section of the path from the Clent Hills to the Lickey Hills and then back to Clent, around 18 miles.

I was at a point in my journey and search for intimacy with God where I needed to share with someone I could trust. I wanted to be able to offload everything if I possibly could, including the bad bits, and not just the things I could easily handle. "Confess your faults one to another" (James 5:16 AV) was a verse of Scripture on my mind at the time, driving me so much that it became essential for me to share the stuff that was painful. "No pain, no gain", as they say. I desperately needed to get things off my chest regardless, even if there was no other reason than the preservation of my own sanity.

We parked the vehicle on the Clent Hills car park and proceeded to walk along the path through picturesque countryside, heading towards Waseley Country Park. It was a

CHAPTER FOUR

fine day and there were very many people out walking that day. It appeared as though there was an endless procession of walkers coming at us from the opposite direction. People on their own, couples, small parties and even groups of ramblers were among those we greeted along the way. We walked and talked together and I shared some of the mess I had got myself into.

Martyn listened intently and then began to share with me the way that sometimes he prayed. He spoke of praying without words and focusing upon Jesus Christ and using the imagination to pray, which really amounted to 'waiting on God'. Instead of controlling the prayer oneself, he advised letting the Holy Spirit take you and letting Him orchestrate the prayer. This was the philosophy of this particular type of prayer (if 'philosophy' is the right word). I began to weep. In a few moments I was sobbing uncontrollably and could hardly catch my breath. I had always felt since the early nineteen seventies that prayer was a call upon my life, and no sooner had he begun to speak than I broke down.

We crossed a stile and the path then took us through a long field. I was crying uncontrollably as we walked through that field, sobbing my heart out and that's not too much of an exaggeration because afterwards my chest ached literally for several hours. I'm amazed at the grace of God every time I think about that day. Considering the number of people we encountered along the way as we walked and talked together, we never met a single soul during the time I was crying.

What Martyn talked about was exactly what I needed to hear. The time we spent together that day was precious and very profitable. It was indeed a further turning point for me and so we made arrangements to meet up a few days later to wait upon God together.

When we met several days later we waited upon God for

about one and a half hours. Afterwards we shared with each other what we had seen, what God had spoken to our hearts, or maybe a revelation that God had given to us. Something clicked inside me and I began to practise this type of prayer at home the way Martyn had taught me.

In the broken state that I was in at that time, I would often cry myself to sleep. Even though there was now a sound awareness of God in the business venture and a feeling of breakthrough which was having a profound effect upon me, there was a deep sense of sorrow, grief and mourning. Some things had changed dramatically but others had not. The addiction to booze was too strong for me to break and the fantasies, visions and pornography had a powerful hold upon me. The strong perception of my own sinfulness was overpowering and sometimes I'd be too scared to fall asleep for fear that I'd wake up and find myself in Hell. No joke!

One evening, a day or so after our prayer time together, I decided to go to bed early to wait upon God and maybe cry myself to sleep as I often did. I sat in bed propped up with pillows and began to focus my attention upon Jesus Christ. No sooner had I begun to reach out internally than

He appeared at the foot of my bed.

I cannot be certain whether the vision was before my eyes or in my imagination — external, internal or both. The vision was black and white; there were no colours. He was clothed in light, bright light — but as I stared it became clear that He was the light itself. I couldn't see His exact features for the light veiled His face, but I knew who He was. Oh, yes, I knew who He was!

I was terrified. I knew that He knew all about me. The light of his eyes saw straight through me and it was obvious that He knew what was going on in my heart and mind. I expected Him to say something to expose my sins or to challenge the evil

CHAPTER FOUR

within me. To put it colloquially, I did actually think that my number was up. But He said nothing to condemn me or otherwise. He came instead and embraced me and we wept together on each other's shoulders. Like the prodigal son of the Bible, I had come home.

When He embraced me it was dynamite! I felt the love, I felt the grace, I felt the purity, and I felt the Holiness like an electric shock passing through my body. When I embraced Him my arms passed straight through Him. He hadn't come to me in flesh and bones but in pure Spirit, nevertheless, the effect upon me was as though He had. His tears cut me up — I thought that my heart would surely break. I cried profusely and sobbed uncontrollably.

His embrace and His weeping meant far more to me than mere words, or even anything that this world could offer. I think I'm correct in saying, I felt for the first time in my entire life, that someone really understood me and that someone really cared. The Son of God loved me so much as to come and embrace me and sit with me in my muck tip and on my dung-hill. He could not have given me anything more precious than that.

Through my sobs I asked, "Why are you doing this?" He lifted His head from off my shoulder and looked me straight in the eye. The brightness of His eyes pierced me through as He said, "It's grace, Rob. It's grace, just grace."

I don't remember if He said anything else that night. I rather fancy that He did but for sure He never mentioned my sins or the evil that I was so conscious of in the depth of my innermost being. That night I did cry myself to sleep but not like before. I don't know whether it was in reality or whether it was fanciful but that night I fell asleep in the Saviour's arms.

5

Steps to Recovery

> Eternity breaks upon the soul
> His design to make you whole
> Be real, dear soul, with God be real
> Don't try to run — nothing conceal
> In prayer, let Jesus be your goal.
>
> *Rob Giles 2010*

Almost every day for the next three months the Lord Jesus came to me in a vision or dream, bearing His pearls of wisdom to bring about the change in my life necessary for healing. I was expecting an instant deliverance; however, that was not to be the case. From that very first visitation it took thirteen months for the alcohol addiction to be broken and even then the victory seemed to be so very, very flimsy.

For me to walk in anything that resembled freedom and victory regarding the other issues I faced, took a great deal longer; and again I knew that I could go back at any time. Victory and freedom is a moment by moment trust in God. However, it does not depend upon us and our efforts. It depends upon Him holding us; my trust was in that.

There were many things He said to me during that period of time and there was much I saw in the visions and received in the dreams which I cannot speak about. It would not be seemly

CHAPTER FIVE

or appropriate for me to do so. So I shall share only what I consider to be relevant: Firstly, the visions that reveal the greatness, goodness and mercy of God, for this will be encouraging. Secondly, the messages He divulged that helped to reshape my thinking, for this will no doubt be helpful to others. Thirdly, the way in which He dealt with me in my journey to freedom, for God will undoubtedly deal with us. He'll deal with you differently from me, but deal with us He will.

It was my wrong thinking and bad choices that had contributed to my descent into spiritual and mental enslavement. So I disclose these things in the hope that what I reveal might be helpful to those who are facing such difficulties and issues of their own.

The evening following that very first visitation, the Lord Jesus came again and stood at the bottom of my bed. He told me: "Your mind is shot." And I marvelled at His choice of words, but what He said only confirmed to me what I already suspected; that my mind was indeed damaged. He continued, "But I'm going to change your way of thinking. Don't be afraid, just trust me; we will work through this together."

"Just trust me" was a phrase that He would subsequently use often and was for me a **very** great encouragement.

Faith terrified me. It seemed to me to be something "big out there" that I did not possess. Of course I admired the people who had it and those who said they had it, but as for me, I would say, "I don't have faith; if I did I could believe God and I would be free." "Only believe!"... wasn't that what they said at Church? This, rightly or wrongly, was my reasoning. Faith seemed to be something beyond my reach. Call it stupid or childish if you will, but when the Saviour said to me: "Trust Me," I somehow felt that I could.

He told me that sometimes I would still be like a mental

cripple and walk with a 'mental limp' so that I would have to trust Him; "My grace is sufficient for you" (2 Corinthians 12:9). The healing of my mind was not going to be perfect and it appeared to me as if it would be a thorn in my side. All of this very much sounded like being hampered to me; I really could have done without all that. Nevertheless, if it would bring the intimacy and presence of God I longed for, then I'd be prepared to go along with it. At least this way there would be less chance of my thinking the victory was my own; the victory would then always be God's. This was very important to me but don't ask me why, because I don't really know. I only know that I greatly valued the thought of being 'kept' by the power of God. That, I think, is its significance.

"Do you want the easy way or the hard way?"

"I can choose?" I questioned, and immediately thought to myself, 'Oh no! Don't give me a choice,' and then rapidly changed my mind because I knew that He knew what I was thinking.

"You choose," I replied; but I already knew what the answer was before He spoke. That was the frightening bit.

"I'll take you the hard way; you'll have to fight for everything you get. But I'll take you the easy way into my presence — just one thought and you'll be with me."

I was unsure what that meant or what I should think, or even how to respond, particularly regarding the bit about "the hard way". It appeared to me that there would be neither miraculous nor instant healing of my mind, or any instant deliverance from the pornographic visions, nor indeed instant freedom from alcohol. Yet He would make His presence instantly available to me. That was the morsel I reached out to grab, or should I say it reached out and took hold of me and made me feel as though everything He was revealing to me was a good deal.

CHAPTER FIVE

Then He said and did something that surprised me. "I could heal your mind just like that." And at that He clicked His fingers. "But I'm not going to. I'm going to take you on a journey through it. We'll go through this together and you will overcome."

"There's a door opened in your mind," He continued, "and I'm not going to close that door, I'm going to use it for Heavenly vision." I knew instantly that the impediments of my mind were the result of a door that had been opened to demonic activity. I've used the word 'mind' here but the Lord Jesus actually used the word 'psyche'. I used 'mind' because it's easily understood; it means the same as psyche but may not appear quite as alarming. This is what the Lord said to me. "There's a door opened in your psyche." He pronounced the 'e' at the end. I didn't know at the time whether that was correct English, but that was what He said and the way He said it. I was not alarmed and understood perfectly at that moment what He meant. Later I looked up the word in the Oxford Dictionary. The word 'psyche' means: "mind or soul". (The Oxford Quick Reference Dictionary p. 723).

Next morning in my Bible reading I came across this verse in Luke's Gospel: "By your patience possess your souls" (Luke 21:19). In my Bible sometimes a word is highlighted and in the margin there appears a profile of the original New Testament Greek word. 'Psuche' was that Greek word profiled from which comes the English word 'psyche' and was translated in Luke 21:19 as **'souls'**.

The meaning given in the margin was as follows: "The seat of the affections, will, desire, emotions, mind, reason and understanding." (Spirit-Filled Life Bible p. 1557). It is, of course, the root from which our word 'psychology' is derived. This satisfied me and was a great comfort to me, confirming my understanding of Christ's words to me. My thinking had been impaired and my mind damaged, and a door to my soul was opened to demonic activity. Now at that precise moment however, there was an acute awareness that God was on my case. I was no longer on my own.

That night the Lord came again. I was struggling with the fantasies and didn't know what to do. I think somehow, I still expected some instant deliverance, particularly since the Lord Jesus Christ was standing there at the foot of my bed only feet away.

"Close the door, Rob," He said to me, "close the door to your thoughts."

"I can do that?" I questioned.

"Yes, you can do that. Trust me; just trust me."

In that moment, there was a 'knowing'. It's almost as though I knew what He was going to say as He spoke and He certainly knew what I was going to say long before I formed the words. I knew that He knew and He knew that I knew. There with the Son of God I was real; real with Him and, more importantly, real with myself. While my thoughts were still forming, even before I spoke, He answered. I stood completely open and vulnerable in the presence of the eternal Son. There was nothing I could hide from Him, and there was certainly nowhere I could run. He knew my every thought before I even thought it.

In the presence of eternity (eternity is the best word to describe the essence of this visitation) there appeared to be time for me to think before I spoke, and plenty of time to catch my thoughts; at least that is how it felt. In everyday life our transactions can happen so quickly that often there seems to be no time between the thought and the deed. One can race from one action to another or from sentence to sentence, totally unaware that a specific thought has to trigger whatever we say, do or feel. If we could but catch that thought we may perhaps

CHAPTER FIVE

change the course of our actions for the better, in what we say and in the way we say it.

Here in the Heavenly vision, however, the thought came and there was **time** for me to process and filter the thought through the eyes of truth and to weigh it against Scripture, in order to accept or reject it **before** I spoke. What an amazing concept that was beginning to dawn upon me!

"I have the power to do that?" I questioned the Lord.

"You have the power to do that. Trust me Rob, trust me."

"Wow!" I exclaimed. I could hardly catch my breath. "Blown away", I think we call it where I come from.

I began to wish that it could be like this all of the time. I had been completely unaware that I had the power to close the door on my thoughts and shut them out, particularly since I had tried so hard in the past. I think there was an underlying fear in me of 'trying to do things in my own strength'. This fear held me back and I'm sure it had stopped me from trying to close that door earlier. This fear was based upon a teaching I had heard in Church. "We mustn't do things in our own strength", I heard people say. It's a perfectly true statement but I had misinterpreted it and it had become for me, in this instance, a great hindrance.

I began immediately to try to put into practice what the Lord Jesus had told me. After years and years of allowing my thoughts to take their course, to suddenly shut down the fantasies certainly wasn't going to be easy. But the Lord hadn't promised me an easy ride; on the contrary He had said, "You'll have to fight for everything you get." The thoughts came constantly and bombarded my mind. The temptation to fantasise was heavy and seemed to be far worse than it had been before. It was as though the heat had suddenly been turned up since the Lord had spoken to me. Worse or not, the thoughts came and I tried to bat them off, seeking to find some Scripture to quote as I closed the door to shut them out. This I did as best I could with some success and many failures. To be truthful, after a while there were far more successes than failures. Things were changing and changing dramatically.

One of the worst times of the day for me was when I awoke. This was one of the times when my thoughts got the better of me. As I lay there in a daze, half asleep and half awake, my mind would wander and the fantasies would begin. This was when I had no control of my thoughts and I could not bat them off or close the door no matter how hard I tried. And I did try. Oh yes, I tried. I strove desperately to stop the thoughts, but I could not.

The Lord Jesus came again a couple of nights later. During the course of our conversation I took courage and said to Him, "I can't control my mind when I wake up."

He replied: "When you wake up and the fantasies begin, get up. Go downstairs and make a cup of tea, sit in the armchair and meet with me there. I'll sustain you. You don't have to do anything or say anything; just focus on me. If something happens, fine. If nothing happens it's still fine — don't worry about it, just turn up."

That phrase "just turn up" seemed to be inspiring to me. He wasn't looking for me to do something great but just 'turn up'. I thought, 'I can do that.'

Next morning, it was still dark when I was conscious of being awake. The fantasies had already begun. When I became fully aware of what was going on I got out of bed and went downstairs and made a cup of tea as the Lord had told me. It was 4.00 a.m. 'Oh dear!' I thought to myself, 'it's a little early isn't it? ... Oh well, in for a penny, in for a pound.' It's a saying we often use locally when we throw caution to the winds. 'Let's do it.'

The Revelatory Visions that Changed My Thinking

6

Two Gems

> Walking along a pebbly beach
> Millions of stones beneath my feet
> But in amongst them unawares
> There are two gemstones lying there
> So simple, ordinary yet grand
> But I may miss them... hidden in sand.
>
> *Rob Giles 2010*

I turned off the light and sat in darkness. As I began to focus upon Christ, trusting the Holy Spirit to guide me and to reach out to Him internally, so He came again and stood before me. This is what He said to me and the subsequent meditation that was triggered by each of His statements.

"I have five things to tell you," He said. "You remember in the 70s..." Instantly my mind was back in the Pentecostal Church setting of that era where my wife and I grew up. "... often you would be facing a trial or difficulty and then in church someone would stand and give a prophetic word. During the course of that message they would declare the Scriptural words: 'Be still and know that I am God.' Or 'Stand still and see the Salvation of God.' You would hear that word and believe, and then in a little while I'd bring you through or bring you out."

That was perfectly true. In those days prophetic words of encouragement were heard often within the Pentecostal framework of worship. I recall visiting a church in Hockley near Birmingham one Saturday night when that line "Be still and know that I am God" rang out (either a prophecy or interpretation of a tongue, I don't remember which). I thought to myself, 'There doesn't seem to be room in the Church for such spontaneous "words of encouragement" these days. You now have to ask permission.' Rightly or wrongly that was my perception at that moment of recollection.

"But I say to you, what about 'being still' all of the time, making it a constant in your life and not just when your back is against the wall?"

I remember saying to the Lord, "What do you mean?" which was an absolutely ridiculous response because at that moment I already knew what He meant. It was as though the statement He made had switched a light on so that I could at last see clearly. In that instant my mind and spirit were alive and experiencing 'being still'. I understood, but there was no time to process it all; He was making His next statement. I was dumbfounded, amazed, elated, everything all at once.

"Again at that time in the 70s," He continued, "you may have been anxious or fearful about something, resulting in being disturbed or disquieted within. At church you often heard a prophetic message of exhortation: 'The Lord says to you, let go; let go, and let God'. You would trust me and release your internal hold. In a very little while I would bring you out or bring you through and you would be rejoicing."

I remember once being in our home Church at Brierley Hill (the Church we attended in those days) when that line was declared: "Let go and let God!" As I sat there in the presence of the Lord Jesus Christ in that Heavenly vision I could even

CHAPTER SIX

name the person who gave that prophetic message.

"But I say to you," He continued, "what about 'letting go' constantly and making 'letting go' a perpetual part of your life?" Then, as though He'd switched on the light once more, I had understanding of what He meant by 'letting go'. Again, it happened so quickly there was no time to process everything; He was moving on to His next point. Nevertheless, I knew that what I had received was within my heart and that I could call upon it whenever necessary.

"The Holy Spirit," He said, "is speaking constantly in the depths of your innermost being, but there is too much going on for you to hear. You are too engrossed in your own agenda, too fast and too busy. There are too many noises and voices without and within, shouting at you, vying for your attention, so that you cannot hear the 'still small voice' of the Spirit or even discern that the voice is there. Slow down! Be still, be quiet and let go. Then you will hear the Spirit of God speaking in your heart to teach and to guide you through your day."

Instantly I saw, I heard, I knew. I cannot think of any other way to describe what was happening within me or around me. Whenever the Lord Jesus spoke during the Heavenly visions, He only had to say two or three words and I saw — sometimes with my eyes and sometimes with my spirit. When He spoke I heard far more than merely the words He said. I heard what He uttered with my ears but I heard far more deep down within the recesses of my being. It is my guess I was hearing with my spirit. I've already put into words elsewhere 'the knowing' that took place whenever He voiced a brief statement.

Nevertheless, I remained myself throughout; there was no change. I hadn't changed miraculously into a 'saint' since He had arrived; I was still the same sinful idiot I was before, having the ability to misinterpret what He said or what was happening. (Try and rationalise the things of the Spirit and you will come unstuck.) "But the natural man does not receive the things of the Spirit of God" (1 Corinthians 2:14). I could also be a fool in my responses if I so desired, accepting or rejecting whatever He said. This knowledge made me tread very carefully and think through every response that I made, whether thought, word or deed. I was afraid of being a hypocrite; I had to be real and true with myself and with the Lord. I was conscious of the possibility of wearing a mask.

The final piece of enlightenment that governed my reactions and responses was this: He alone was in control of the Heavenly vision. I had to go wherever the vision (or He) took me; I was helpless in this respect. It was only in utter abandonment to Him that I could proceed through each and every Heavenly vision. 'If only I could carry this abandonment through into my everyday life,' I thought to myself. Then it occurred to me, 'Maybe I could if I learnt how to *be still* and to *let go.*'

At that point there flashed before my eyes occasions when I had felt an impulse or impression, like an unspoken 'voice', urging me to do something or respond in a certain way. I hadn't obeyed but it later proved that had I followed the instruction, things might have turned out for the better. Maybe it would even have placed me in a position where I was 'one step ahead'. I realised I'd often had an impression of someone or something speaking to me and later wishing that I had followed the impulse.

I thought of some of the testimonies I'd heard of those who hadn't gone into work the day that terror struck the twin towers on 9/11; of the impulse or the strong impression they received not to go to work that day. There was also a story that came to mind, which I had heard two or three decades previously of a man who was travelling to a certain place. He had a strong feeling or an inner 'voice' urging him not to get on the train.

CHAPTER SIX

He didn't take that train and later he heard on the news that the train had crashed. 'What are you saying to me Lord?' I thought. I sensed that if I were still enough and could let go of my scepticism, I too would hear, take note and possibly obey.

A day or so later I had two occasions to put into action obedience to the 'inner voice' of the Spirit.

I was taking down an old garden fence and replacing it with a construction of some significance: vertical planks were fixed to horizontal cross members which in turn were bolted to six feet high 'godfathers' (concrete posts). The nuts and bolts were badly corroded and had to be ground off with an angle grinder in order to take the fence apart. As I went to my van to get the said angle grinder, I had an impression or inner voice saying to me, "Put your safety gloves on!"

Without questioning I put them on and then merrily proceeded to carry out the task in hand. I got to the stage where I'd removed around a half dozen bolts and then, as I held onto the godfather with my left hand and the angle grinder in my right, the grinding wheel slipped; while still in motion it ran between my two middle fingers and across the palm of my left hand. I dread to think what might have happened if I hadn't obeyed that inner voice and put on the safety gloves. Well, I just danced and praised the Lord; there were no marks on my hand at all.

Later, while using the circular saw to cut through some timber I again heard the inner voice speak to me: "You are going to cut your bench." I stopped and looked down and around the saw. "No, no way," I distinctly remember saying out loud and then continued with my task of sawing the wood and promptly sawed through the bench. "Oh, no!" I exclaimed, "I should have listened to the voice." I knew this was a lesson that was going to take time to learn. This was a revelation sparking a revolution within.

It was from hearing and trying to obey the 'still small voice' that gifts of the Spirit such as the word of wisdom and the word of knowledge were developed, although it did take four or five years before I fully recognised that what was taking place was actually those gifts in action.

Meanwhile, in the vision it was becoming clear that God wanted me to walk in constant communion with Him. For me to hear the voice of the Spirit within was God communing with me. For me to talk to God was me communing with Him, and this I attempted to do as often as I could throughout the day. I saw that real communion was a two-way communication. How had I missed it?

Prayer seemed now to take on a whole new meaning. Getting up early to wait upon God was a great step forward and was coupled with an attempt on my part to listen to the voice of God and to slow myself down and *be still*. I saw there and then that waiting upon God over this last week or so had completely changed my life. I was now hearing things that I'd formerly overlooked. Oh, brother!

I recalled having read somewhere of Smith Wigglesworth and how his life was that of constant communion with God. As a consequence of this perpetual two-way conversation of communion, the very presence of God was manifest wherever he went.

"No doubt it was a result of Smith Wigglesworth's much daily, hourly communion with God that somehow his very presence anywhere created a spiritual atmosphere in which you felt that God was near and that all things were possible." (W. Hacking, *A Life Ablaze with the Power of God*, page 47). I longed to be able to carry the presence of God wherever I went. Smith Wigglesworth's life was one of constant prayer. The Apostle Paul said, "Pray without ceasing" (1 Thessalonians 5:17). I called to mind too the title of a song by Keith Green

CHAPTER SIX

"Make my life a prayer" (from the album *No Compromise*, Sparrow Records 1979), and I thought of that young man's great longing for constant intimacy and communion with God conveyed in the lyrics of many of his songs.

Things were now beginning to fit together. Momentarily I considered the possibility of constant communion with God, which in turn raised a question in my mind: Was it possible for my life to become a constant prayer? The impression I had at that juncture was in the affirmative. This raised an additional question regarding the presence of God. Had God placed His very presence within me? At that instant I had the conviction that He had indeed placed His presence within. 'What a great honour,' I thought to myself, 'to be afforded the privilege of bearing the presence of God! But how on earth am I going to discover it, tap into it and live in it? How!?' That indeed was the question.

At that moment the Lord spoke again and confirmed it to my heart. "The Kingdom of God is within you," He said. "Come, sit and wait with me." He continued, "Be still, let go and plumb the depth of your innermost being and find me there."

I could now see that He was already there in the depth of my being because I was a Christian. If He were there then His presence was there (stating the obvious!). By getting up early in the morning and waiting on God I was *being still* and permitting myself to 'plumb the depth of my inner man' as it were, to find the Christ within. What I now needed to do was allow that stillness to permeate my entire being and take it with me throughout the rest of my day. That would change my life.

The reality was now dawning upon me and I began to feel the impact in every fibre of my being. God had placed within me His presence. If I were still or quiet enough I would hear the 'still small voice' of the Spirit communing with me in the depth of my heart. If I were *still* every moment and if I were to constantly *let go* of my inhibitions and stuff that held me back, it would be possible to live every moment in the presence of God. This then was the way in which I could 'tap into' and 'live in' the presence of the Almighty. Undoubtedly this was to me an awesome discovery.

I thought of the book by Brother Lawrence, "Practicing the Presence of God," a book of the utmost simplicity that invites and teaches the reader to do just as the title says. 'I must get another copy of that book and read it again,' I thought. 'I remember lending it out but I don't think I've had it back.'

Next I was thinking of another aspect of being still, that of serenity. I'd witnessed this in the lives of only a few people — people who were unfazed by life's circumstances. I came across the following little story which illustrates this serenity, again from the life of Smith Wigglesworth.

"One blustery morning we started up the lane, for the usual short walk. Brother Wigglesworth, getting on in years, walked with measured steps. Turning left at the end of the lane, we climbed a steep incline in the road which brought us to a humpback bridge spanning the canal. The wind was blowing things in all directions. Brother Wigglesworth was always immaculately dressed, and this particular morning he was wearing a smart new cap which obviously had cost quite a bit of money. Just as we reached the summit of the bridge, a great gust of wind lifted his new cap and blew it off his head and into the canal. I have often said that if that cap had been mine, I would have been diving into the canal to retrieve it. Not Brother Wigglesworth. Without turning an eyelid, he quietly turned round and said, 'We had better go back, Brother Hacking. I can't go walking out on a day like this without a cap on my head.' Perfect calm..." (W. Hacking, *A Life Ablaze with the Power of God*, page 53).

CHAPTER SIX

This was the serenity I longed for. I was now seeing endless possibilities stemming from the practice of 'being still'. As it says in the Psalms, "Meditate within your heart... and be still" (Psalm 4:4) and again, "Be still and know that I am God" (Psalm 46:10). These are verses like signposts that show the way. 'Could it be possible,' I thought, 'that they reveal the way into what the Apostle Paul longed for when he said, "that I might know Him and the power of His resurrection"?' (Philippians 3: 10)

Three things were now clear to me. Firstly, *being still* would allow me time to process what was going on before I made any decision as to what to say or what to do (isn't this what James meant when he said, "be swift to hear, slow to speak"? James 1:19). This was just as it was in the Heavenly vision I had seen only a few days previously (the apparent sense of unlimited time and space). When Wigglesworth's hat blew off he was unhurried, quiet and still inside. He appeared to have time in that one moment to think, to 'let go' of any automatic reaction and to make a calculated response.

Secondly, being still would lead me into rest. As the Scripture says in the book of Hebrews, "There remains therefore a rest for the people of God" (Hebrews 4: 9). I concluded that it would be impossible for me to enter into 'the rest of the Lord' without being still. After all, if I were at rest then I would be enjoying the serenity I longed for. The one would lead naturally into the other. Stillness, rest and serenity are all inextricably linked.

Thirdly, stillness would draw me deeper into God. The reality of "the Kingdom of God is within you", coupled with the words of Paul: "... in Him we live and move and have our being" (Acts 17: 28) could be summed up in these words: GOD IS IN ME AND GOD IS ALL AROUND ME. By being still and letting go, I could allow myself to be conscious of that truth constantly. God in me and all around me did not depend on whether or not I 'felt' that I was living in His presence. It did not depend on feelings; it depended on what Christ had said and whether or not I believed it.

The *letting go* seemed to be powerful. The less I held onto, the better. My selfish motives and wanting my own way were but two areas in which I could let go. Then the Lord said to me, "Letting go amounts to nothing less than SURRENDER." 'Surrender' was a word that also terrified me just as 'Faith' had. I knew my life wasn't surrendered to God (at least that is how I felt); even though in prayer I had often given everything to Him. If I were surrendered to God I would be living for God totally, but I'm not. That was my logic, rightly or wrongly. I could see that I was the problem and that the problem was within. I had often given things to God but had promptly taken them back; at least that's how it all appeared to me. In reality I simply hadn't let go. In the presence of Christ, however, I felt that I could let go. Those words that Jesus spoke to me, that 'letting go' amounted to surrender, were staggering when I thought about them; but very true.

After this encounter, I began to look up a few Scriptures with the aid of a concordance in order to piece things together. I remember being surprised as I looked at the clock. It was 6.30 a.m. — two and a half hours had flown by as if they were a moment. It was time to get ready for work. I shared briefly with Maureen what had happened and then set off for work to hang a few doors for a customer.

7

A Change of Mind ...
A Change of Heart

> To have a change of heart
> You first must change your mind
> All the thoughts you dwell on
> Will rule you every time
> Whatever things are lovely
> Pure, and just, and clean
> Is any thing of good report?
> Then think upon these things
>
> *Rob Giles 2010*

Throughout this period of 'visitation', I was meeting with Mary Noott, an elderly lady from the Church my wife and I were attending. Mary was, and still is, a very close friend to both of us and we love her very dearly. Mary is one of those ladies of spiritual maturity that people sought out for her guidance and admonition. Frequently I would speak to her on the phone to share with her what God was doing in my life and to drink in her wise counsel.

More often than not I'd make the call around 8 o'clock in the morning, usually upon arrival at work. She was so busy during that phase of her life it was probably the only time of day I'd be virtually guaranteed to reach her. There was a telephone by her bedside and generally speaking she'd still be in bed when I called. Nevertheless, she never complained or objected to my calling her so early in the day. I'm very grateful to her for that; I really needed to share these things with someone else as well as with Maureen.

The day following the early morning encounter with the Lord Jesus where He had said to me, "Letting go amounts to nothing less than SURRENDER," I was due to finish work early. Accordingly I arranged to see Mary at her home. We talked and shared with each other over a cup of tea and I disclosed the vision and what the Lord had shown me regarding the importance of 'being still' and 'letting go'. I recall, at some point in our conversation, saying to her, "The Lord promised five things He was going to show me. So far He's shown me only two."

"You can revisit a vision," she answered.

I already sensed I needed to return one way or another to the vision; her reply added momentum to my resolve.

"Yes," I said thoughtfully, "looks like that's what I'm gonna have to do."

Next morning I rose early to wait upon God, somewhere around 4.00 a.m. Not many minutes into my prayer the Lord Jesus came again and stood before me in the vision. He didn't say much in this vision but what He did say released many Scriptures into my mind.

What I am about to say may seem nonsensical, but one must bear in mind that I was not 'in the natural'. I have touched on this before but it is worth repeating. This was a moment in which the 'supernatural', 'heaven', 'eternity' (whatever you want to call it) had broken in upon me and things do not take place in a normal fashion at such times. What I 'heard' was not necessarily what the Lord said to me. In the vision I often 'heard' the message yet not always with my ears. Neither did it come from the Saviour's lips; it was all around me

CHAPTER SEVEN

(hearing with the spirit no doubt). The narrative is also about what I 'saw' but not essentially what I saw with my eyes. Time and again I 'saw' from within, in the depth of my being (seeing with the spirit). This is difficult to convey and the vision is difficult to describe; so I have written it as one might write a sequence of meditative thoughts in a journal.

I also reveal my conclusions in this account, which came naturally and flowed with ease and clarity. One doesn't have to be an expert in the powers of deduction to arrive at such decisive reasoning, certainly not in a Heavenly vision. This may appear contradictory to what I said in the previous chapter, but it is not; it is the paradox of visionary understanding. I think I could have been a simpleton, a buffoon, the village idiot or even a mannequin and still I'd be able to comprehend what was unfolding before me! That is genuinely how I felt in this vision; there was always a sense of my own weakness and limitation, yet throughout an overwhelming feeling of the limitlessness of the One who stood before me. The understanding is *given* but our will to *choose* remains firmly in our own hands, either to accept or reject.

"Change your mind Rob, change your mind," the Lord said to me as He took me by the hand. "This is repentance." Straight away across my mind, possibly even my vision, flashed a couple of verses from the Amplified Bible. The first related to John the Baptist which reads as follows:
"John the Baptist appeared in the wilderness (desert), preaching a baptism [obligating] repentance (a change of one's mind for the better, heartily amending one's ways, with abhorrence of past sins). — Mark 1:4 (The Amplified Bible).

The second piece of Scripture from the Amplified Bible was associated with Jesus Christ Himself:
"Jesus came into Galilee, preaching the good news (the Gospel) of the Kingdom of God, and saying, 'The [appointed period of]

time is fulfilled (completed), and the Kingdom of God is at hand; repent' (have a change of mind which issues in regret for past sins and in a change of conduct for the better)" Mark 1:15 (The Amplified Bible).

These (Amplified Bible) Scriptures contained the definition of repentance, reinforcing the message Christ was communicating to me that repentance is essentially a change of mind. This is in fact the meaning of the New Testament Greek word translated 'repent'.

"What about making repentance a constant in your life," He continued, "and constantly changing your mind for the better and aligning your thoughts to my purpose?"

"I've tried as often as I can to ask God for forgiveness and say sorry for the things I've done wrong," I said (as much to myself as to the Lord).

"Repentance is not about saying sorry," He replied. This rocked me and shook me to the very core.

When I had regained my poise, I briefly considered the facts. I had often said "sorry" and then gone away and done the very thing I'd just said "sorry" for. That did not appear to be repentance to me. "You're right," I said thoughtfully. To which the Lord answered; "Repentance is a change of mind which in turn brings about a change in behaviour."

"As he thinks in his heart, so is he" (Proverbs 23:7) was a Scripture that pierced my senses, establishing beyond any doubt that all of my actions were prompted by a definite thought. To live my life in repentance was to perpetually 'change my mind' and align my thinking with God's; but I would need to *be still* in order to do that.

This then was my conclusion in the light of what I was seeing and hearing in these revelatory visions. Whenever I was conscious that I'd sinned I was to stand *still* internally and *let go* (which added up to 'release' and 'surrender'), *change my*

CHAPTER SEVEN

mind (repent) and *thank God*. I had no idea where the 'thank God' came from; it seemed to be out of keeping with what I was seeing and hearing. Nevertheless, it was something I needed to do 'instinctively'. Then I heard the Lord Jesus say, "... and then, unruffled, move on with God as though nothing had happened."

"You are joking, right?" I said out loud (I was querying and not speaking to the Lord disparagingly).

"Do you think it PLEASES me when you punish yourself for days after you've fallen?" Jesus questioned me in reply. This was definitely what I did with regard to the booze and the pornographic fantasies. After the indulgence I would punish myself and grieve over the fall for days afterwards. Pride and shame were very great hindrances and I could now see that they were impostors.

"It GRIEVES ME when you torture yourself," He continued, "because I have provided the way out."

Instantly across my sight there burst several verses from the Bible: "He has delivered us from the power of darkness and conveyed us into the Kingdom of the Son of His love, in whom we **have** redemption through his blood, the **forgiveness of sins**." (Colossians 1:13 & 14) and also Ephesians 1:7, "In him we **have** redemption through his blood, the **forgiveness of sins**, according to the riches of his grace." I've emboldened the words that came with emphasis.

At that precise moment, I was arrested by the fact there were no New Testament Scriptures to teach us that we should 'beg' or 'grovel' to God for forgiveness; we had it already through His blood.

"Reach out and take it, Rob!" the Lord Jesus said to me.

I wanted to say, "How?" but that was ridiculous because I instantly knew the answer. I would be reaching out to take hold of it if I adopted, in one move, the principles outlined to me.

Namely, to let go, change my mind (repent), give thanks to God and then, unruffled, move on with God as though nothing had happened.

The 'unruffled and move on as though nothing had happened' bit, was huge to me because I knew I'd have to lay aside my pride and let go of my shame in order to perform such an exercise. At times these two, pride and shame, were very subtle, so natural and normal they had become indiscernible — virtually undetectable. Pride was more than mere arrogance, "I'm not going to lower myself to perform that". But it was one aspect of the pride I saw in myself which made me shudder.

Shame, I discerned, was a comfort to me, albeit a perverse source of comfort. It was also a crutch — but a crutch that (without my knowledge) had snapped and pierced my armpit, so to speak. It was also a justifier. I felt justified in feeling the way I did; the same too could be said of pride. Nevertheless, if I wanted to get through this mess and go hand in hand with God, I'd have to break through the shame barrier and move on. A day or so later I had the occasion to prove it.

Following the walk with Martyn, it had become my custom to rise early to pray. As it happened I had a sleep disorder — no trouble getting to sleep but staying asleep was the problem. Rather than let it get me down, I decided to use the sleep disorder to my advantage, enabling me to get up and pray in the 'watches of the night'. The Lord had told me to get out of bed and go and meet with Him whenever my mind started to wander.

This particular morning I did not rise and very soon my mind was out of my control. I could not shake it and I sank to depths I'd rather not remember. Afterwards I was filled with shame and regret. Shame covered my face and I was riddled with guilt as I sat in the chair. I asked the Lord to forgive me and prayed all the 'bemoaning my state' prayers I could conjure

CHAPTER SEVEN

up.

The Lord spoke to me, "Reach out and take my hand." I could pray prayers of anguish, of sorrow, of regret and bemoaning my state with the greatest of ease but I could not pray with the thought that He was standing there in person and then move on as though nothing had happened. Not at that moment. Not after I'd just sinned. Perhaps I might be able to in a day or two's time when I'd got over it or when the feelings had worn off. Why was that? Well, it was guilt and shame.

'Oh dear,' I said to myself. Just the very thought of pressing through, in spite of the shame, seemed so incredibly painful. This was for me the first time I had ever made an attempt to *let go* and *unruffled move on*. I could literally feel the pain. It was rather like a hot poker searing my brain or my emotions being torn with a bear's claw. When you are consumed by guilt and shame and someone is pressing you to push through to believe, regardless of the way you feel, you will want to slap them and scream in no uncertain terms: "Get lost!" or something similar!! Just the thought of pressing through regardless was like a burning sensation through my mind, which left me with the feeling that I would tear myself apart if I did 'let go and unruffled move on'.

I could not think rationally. Guilt and shame had dulled my senses. They had blinded my understanding, dominated my thinking and governed my responses, and I was left with an overwhelming feeling of inadequacy. I had a deep sense of inferiority and felt utterly rejected and dejected. I had become very withdrawn.

Guilt and shame were massive obstacles to confront and they had become a very great hindrance to my recovery. Which shows just how powerful and destructive guilt and shame can be. What is more, I had suffered and endured the damage that guilt and shame could cause for the biggest part of my life.

Nevertheless I knew that these two emotions were in some way essential to my recovery.

In reality guilt and shame are both friend and foe; hindrance and necessity, without which, we would not be aware of our condition. We would not be aware of our wrong doing, nor would we be aware of our need for a Saviour. Guilt and shame are in fact a gift from God to lead us to Christ, for we only have the right to let them go before God because Jesus took both our guilt and our shame upon Himself on the cross. To attempt to shake off and eradicate guilt and shame, unless we are able to do so in the full knowledge that Jesus Christ bore them on the cross, is in my view a mistake. For if we are not careful, what little bit of conscience we do have will be tossed aside and we will end up with hardened hearts.

When we accept that Jesus bore our guilt and shame on the cross and we confess our sins, we put ourselves in a powerful position where we can freely receive the forgiveness of God. God's response to us is always with grace — propelled into action by Love and is summed up in this verse of Scripture: "For God so loved the world that He gave His only begotten Son, that whoever believes in Him should not perish but have everlasting life." (John 3:16).

I knew that the Holy Spirit was urging me to 'let it go' and to press through. Everything within me seemed to be screaming, "THIS IS WRONG" and I wanted desperately to give up and return to my old PASSIVE way. However, I was constrained to make the choice to let go from within, and so make a determined attempt to move on as though nothing had happened. From within I reached out to take the hand of Christ (as he had instructed me). To my utter astonishment and almost disbelief, He was there before me in the vision. I was guilt-ridden but He spoke to me as though nothing had happened. He had forgiven and forgotten. 'So quickly?' I thought to myself,

CHAPTER SEVEN

'This cannot be!' In actual fact, I was the one who couldn't forgive myself, neither could I instantly forget.

After that experience I began to adopt the principles He had shown me. Namely, to let go, change my mind (repent), give thanks to God and then, unruffled, move on with God as though nothing had happened. I adopted this pattern not only in my conflict with the pornographic fantasies and visions but also in my quest to combat and overcome the alcohol problem. It was not easy, but one way or another I had to live with God in each moment. This was an amazing lesson, a revelation that sparked a further revolution in me.

8

Repentance
(in a way I'd never seen before)

Standing in the doorway where you've fallen thrice before
Many enticing pleasures beckon to you once more
Once across this threshold there'll be no turning back
So now's the time to turn and run and never to look back.

Rob Giles 2010

In a vision the following morning the Lord Jesus came again and this time He lifted me up by the hand. We walked and talked together and then He launched straight into where He had left off the previous day.

"What about repenting before you sin?"

"Hey!" I exclaimed. It was as though He'd tossed a grenade into my rationale. His words had brought me up sharply and shattered my train of thought. "You're joking!"

"Not at all," He replied. And then in front of my eyes literally (a vision within a vision) I saw a verse from the Bible being divided; that's the only way I can describe it. A gap was emerging in the text.

The verse turned out to be James 1:14 although I didn't know it at the time. In fact none of the verses of Scripture I saw or heard in any vision came with chapter and verse; I looked

CHAPTER EIGHT

them up afterwards just to check them out and make sure they were 'kosher' as people say.

The verse began, "But each one is tempted when he is drawn away by his own desires." That was a shock to me. "The Scripture said 'own desires'!" I exclaimed almost out loud. "The problem therefore comes from within; I must be the problem. Nobody ever taught me that before. I'd always thought it was the devil."

Dumbfounded, I thought to myself, 'We have a tendency to blame the devil for something that is innate.' (I did actually use the word 'we'; I don't think I was quite ready at that point to take full responsibility for myself and use the word 'I'.) I was still ducking and diving!

The next two words read, "... and enticed".

"Oh, so that's where the devil comes in!" I exclaimed. "He does the enticing!"

I read on. "Then, when desire has conceived, it gives birth to sin; and sin, when it is full-grown, brings forth death."

"That's where you repent," the Lord said. And then before my eyes I saw that gap which I've mentioned emerging in the text. There was a literal separation taking place between the words 'desire' and 'conceived'.

"That's where you change your mind, between the desire and the conception of the sin; that's where you repent."

"No one ever taught me this in Church!" I gasped again aloud. There was no rebuke; it was more important that I grasped the truth He was conveying to me. I was knocked sideways by what I'd seen. Imagine if you will, a pauper suddenly discovering that he or she is the sole beneficiary of a vast estate. That is pretty much the way I felt throughout this vision. It was rather like unearthing hidden treasure although I cannot claim any of these conclusions to be my own. I didn't have the mental prowess of reason and intelligence at that stage of my journey.

The separation I saw taking place in the text of James 1:14, between the 'desire' and the 'conception' began to reveal to me something about 'separation' I'd never seen before — how there was an inseparable link to repentance.

I had come from a Pentecostal background and 'separation' was one of the major doctrines in the Pentecostal tradition. It was something I had longed for but could not find a route to achieve it in a way that worked for me. Now, surprisingly, I saw it, and it was within easy reach.

By changing my mind at that crucial moment of temptation (between the desire and the conception), just as I'd seen the separation taking place in the text, I too would be bringing about a separation within myself. Through the constant *changing of my mind* in favour of God's way I would, as the Scriptures say, be 'renewing my mind'. I would be putting off the old — my rubbish — and putting on the new — the Lord's best. I would indeed be putting on 'the mind of Christ'. Repenting, or having a change of mind, at that crucial moment of temptation between the 'desire' and the 'conception' would cut off the sin and stop it dead in its tracks. Slowly but surely as I persistently cut off the sin, the 'separation to God' I so greatly desired would be delivered. Separation would then be a journey, an ongoing process, rather than the instant portion I had hitherto thought it to be.

Just the notion that I'd be separating myself from the sins that crippled me was incredible and brought with it a great sense of relief, joy and peace (despite the fact that I now realised the victory over crippling sins would not be instant). I would be putting distance between me and the things that held me in their grip. This Scripture came to mind: " 'Come out from among them and be separate,' says the Lord" (2 Corinthians 6:17). Separation was now taking on a whole new

CHAPTER EIGHT

meaning.

"Wow!" I exclaimed out loud, "I've never seen anything like this before." The very thing that had eluded me was at once within my reach; that was beyond belief! I never imagined that I'd be capable of bringing about a 'separation to God' internally. This left me almost breathless. At the same time I knew there had to be a separation externally. I had to distance myself from the things that triggered temptation. I would most certainly be a fool if I were to surround myself with bottles of booze or pictures of scantily clad women. Separation had to be both internal and external. It frightened me to think that some people had a separation that was external only. It's rather like the Pharisees who, in the words of Jesus, were like "whitewashed tombs which indeed appear beautiful outwardly, but inside full of dead men's bones and all uncleanness" (Matt.23:27).

"Be still, Rob," the Lord said to me. "Be still." And at that He raised His hand. My thoughts slowed down in order to reflect. If I were *still* enough and held on to as little as possible of self, I would progressively become more conscious of what was going on within me and around me. This led me to think of something else equally significant — what the Bible calls 'watching' (1 Peter 4:7).

This verse from the Psalms gave clarity: "How shall a young man cleanse his way? By taking heed and keeping **watch** [on himself] according to your word [conforming his life to it]." Psalm 119:9 (The Amplified Bible).

I noticed three things:
• Firstly, the implication of knowing the Scriptures became very clear to me. The verse read "... according to your word". I would never know how God wanted me to act, respond, think or speak, nor would I be able to spot that all-important 'moment' of temptation unless I knew the Word of God.

- Secondly, the worth of watching and what it really meant began to dawn upon me, as given in the verse from Psalm 119:9 of the Amplified Bible: "By taking heed and keeping watch [on himself]." I simply needed to be observant, more aware of what was going on within me and around me, not allowing things to steal in upon me, or overtake me. I wouldn't be able to do this without being *still*. Nor would I spot that all-important 'moment' of temptation unless I 'watched'.

'I've been a Christian for almost thirty-five years and I have no idea what "watching" is all about. Can you believe that?' I said to myself. Then these words that the Lord spoke to his disciples in the Garden of Gethsemane came to me. "Watch and pray, lest you enter into temptation" (Matt. 26:41). 'Watching' too began taking on a whole new meaning from that time onwards. Watching 'according to Your word' became the vehicle enabling me to know when or what to *let go* of, but it was only possible if I slowed down inside and became *still*.

- The third thing I noticed was tied in with the phrase that read: "... according to your word [conforming his life to it]" Psalm 119:9 of the Amplified Bible. To 'conform' one's life to the word would actually entail a *change of mind*, effectuating a change of heart and so transforming one's ways in favour of God's ways. This basically is the Amplified Bible's definition of repentance found in the Gospel of Mark (1:4 and 1:15) — the two Scriptures I had seen a day earlier. I had now gone full circle.

The 'gap' that I saw in the text between the 'desire' and the 'conception' in James 1:14 intrigued me. As I watched, so the gap increased in size. I was catching a glimpse of more space which in turn suggested to me more time. Simultaneously, I was also seeing how I lived in everyday life.

The way in which I lived was virtually habitual; my reactions and responses were spontaneous, quick, unmeasured,

CHAPTER EIGHT

instinctive and automatic. I would need space in which to change my mind. I'd need time; much more time, time that really wasn't there in order to detect that all-important 'moment' of temptation.

I saw and relived an event that had taken place a day or so earlier: I was in the kitchen getting a plate out of a low-level cupboard. There were five or six plates stacked one on top of the other and some dishes on top of the plates. With my left hand I held the dishes back while with my right I pulled the plate out from underneath and unsuspectingly dragged another plate out with it which fell and smashed on the floor. "Oh blast!" — The words were out of my mouth before I knew it. I was so cross as the plate lay in pieces on the floor. "Stupid plate!" I exclaimed and kicked the cupboard door shut, being more annoyed with the plate than with myself. I felt sick. This was an example of my unthinking, automatic and instinctive behaviour. Things had to change. I felt so lost and desolate.

I then saw myself during one of the very first visitations that had occurred several weeks earlier. I experienced once more the amazing sense of 'time' that I had felt in the Heavenly vision. Time to think through my responses before I made them. I became familiar once again with the longing I'd had for that awareness of 'time and space' to continue into my everyday life.

Right there and then I saw and heard the answer I craved, emerging before me as a distinct possibility. The more I slowed down and was still, plus the more I began changing my mind at that all-important moment, the more space I'd be creating for myself. The more I was *still* and *changed my mind*, the more appreciation I'd have of what was going on within me and around me, thus giving the impression of more time in which to make those necessary choices and changes.

Given my mental state at that time (which was manic, to

Repentance (in a way I'd never seen before)

say the least), I now understood the importance of slowing down, of 'stillness' and being quiet within. Further, given the fact that I lived constantly in the realms of my feelings and emotions, I detected the necessity of *letting go*. Somehow I knew that if I embarked upon this journey of repentance with Jesus Christ by my side, there were going to be some dramatic changes. I sensed that it would be at times very painful; it would certainly not be easy. Nevertheless, I also knew it would yield the fruit for which I had so longed.

Immediately after this visitation and vision within a vision, I began to try to practise 'this repentance' before I actually sinned (which we would call resisting). I had to start somewhere, so I chose something that was obvious, something wherein I would easily spot that moment of temptation. 'Ah! Anxiety is a good start,' I thought. 'I'll start there.' Just simply trying to be still helped immensely. To bring about a change of mind when I felt the anxiety (which in actual fact was most of the time, given my manic state of mind), I chose to speak a verse of Scripture to my heart. "Be anxious for nothing, but in everything by prayer and supplication, with thanksgiving, let your requests be made known to God." (Philippians 4:6) I then sought to *let go* of my anxious feeling and *let go* of my internal hold upon it (which together brought about the change of mind) and then move on quietly as though nothing had happened.

Lo and behold, the more I did it and worked on that one habitual response, the more time I appeared to have. This was in stark contrast to my previous behaviour where once I had no time at all because my reactions had been so automatic. Throughout this venture I had to be as calm and as still as a mill pond deep down inside (if I could), which was far easier said than done. But I had no choice; if I wasn't calm and still, I'd miss that moment. I had to let go and hold on to as little of SELF as possible in order to do it. SELF was a major

CHAPTER EIGHT

hindrance; it wasn't easy but when everything came together it worked. The more I was *still* and *changed my mind*, the more 'space' I had, in turn giving the appearance that there was more time. This may sound ridiculous, but it worked. I've often thought, rightly or wrongly, 'Could this be part of what Paul meant when he spoke about "redeeming the time, because the days are evil" (Ephesians 5:16)?' It certainly felt to me as though I was redeeming time!!

However, back in the vision I was seeing some words of the Apostle Paul from the letter to the Romans shooting like flashes of lightning before my eyes; like bullet points in a T.V. commercial penetrating my mind and permeating the depth of my being. Words such as: "But now, it is no longer I who do it, but sin that dwells in me" (Romans 7:17). And "For I know that in me (that is in my flesh) nothing good dwells; for to will is present with me, but how to perform what is good I do not find" (Romans 7:18).

In fact the remainder of chapter 7 started to scroll before my eyes rather like the credits at the end of a movie. I was used to this stuff because it was similar to what took place in many of my demonic fantasy visions.

Every thought, word or deed initiated by the flesh (self) was under the law of SIN and DEATH. They were dead works and as such, not of God. I thought back to the verse I'd seen from the book of James. "And sin, when it is fully grown, brings forth death." With the flesh (self) I could only ever serve the law of SIN. My thoughts were only stating the obvious.

My major problem was not sins, for sins could be forgiven. It was SIN; an indwelling principle which was rooted in SELF and in the FLESH; that was the problem. Further Scriptures from the books of Romans and Galatians came to me regarding 'dying to self'. "For if you live according to the flesh you will die; but if by the Spirit you put to **death** the deeds of the body, you will live. For as many as are led by the Spirit of God, these are the sons of God" (Romans 8:13 & 14). By changing my mind at that crucial moment, I would be slowly putting to death the deeds of the body. 'Wow! That was awesome,' I said to myself; and then the Scriptures continued: "Knowing this, that our old man was crucified with Him, that the body of sin might be done away with, that we should no longer be slaves of sin" (Romans 6:6). And then Galatians 2:20 which reads: "I have been crucified with Christ; it is no longer I that live, but Christ lives in me; and the life which I now live in the flesh I live by faith in the Son of God, who loved me and gave Himself for me."

It appeared from these verses that 'dying to self' was the only way that I could get free. Somehow, 'self' needed to die so that Christ could live in me. I felt exposed, almost naked in His presence. I felt as though I stood in the shoes of Paul when he said: "O wretched man that I am! Who will deliver me from this body of death?" (Romans 7:24)

I read on: "I thank God — through Jesus Christ our Lord!" I'd heard this preached many times before but never adequately enough for me to see the mechanics of it — how it worked. I thought to myself, 'Never were we shown how to lay hold of this victory in Christ and make it workable, moment by moment.'

Notwithstanding the wealth of revelation I was receiving, I wasn't ready for the final statement: "So then, with the **mind** I myself serve the law of God, but with the flesh the law of sin" (Rom. 7:25). I stared open-mouthed. My eyes then turned away from what I was seeing and glanced at the Lord who was standing a little to one side. I then turned to gawp once more at that statement of Scripture before, still open-mouthed, turning finally to gaze at the Lord of Glory as if to say "Can this be?"

CHAPTER EIGHT

But He answered before I even got those words out of my mouth.

"Yes! It's true."

The 'changing of the mind' at that moment of temptation would work Christ's victory within. "So then with the MIND I myself serve the law of God." This was staggering!

"Can I really do this?" I questioned. Everything appeared to make sense.

"You can do it. Trust me Rob, just trust me."

9

Trust and Obey

> You know that you must trust Him
> You know you must believe
> Obedience is not magic
> No cards tucked up your sleeve
> No vanishing assistants
> No rabbits out of hats
> You only need obey Him
> And trustingly believe.
>
> *Rob Giles 2010*

When the Lord said those words to me, "Trust me Rob. Trust me," it was the moment when I became aware that trust was the positive action to follow a positive change of mind. Then He said, "What about trusting me constantly?" That appeared to be the natural thing to do if the previous three things He'd spoken to me about were constants in my life. It would provide a massive shift from the self-absorption of my depression. To actually look away from myself and look to someone else would be frightening but truly amazing.

This verse of Scripture came before me: "As you therefore have received Christ Jesus the Lord, so walk in Him" (Colossians 2:6). This verse answered any question I may have had as to how I should live my life in Christ: "As you have received Him"!

CHAPTER NINE

"How did I first receive Christ?" Before I'd got the words out of my mouth the answer was there, summed up in this verse: "Repent and believe the Gospel" (Mark 1:15). I saw the verse from a standard translation and I also saw it from the Amplified Bible which contained a definition of 'repent' and 'believe' which reads as follows:
"Repent (have a change of mind which issues in regret for past sins and in a change of conduct for the better) and believe (trust in, rely on, and adhere to) the good news (the Gospel)." (Mark 1:15 The Amplified Bible).

The way in which I had first received Jesus Christ into my life was simply by 'repenting' and 'believing'. If I were to apply that to Colossians 2:6, my day-to-day walk with God would be the same: repent and believe — nothing more — nothing less. 'How on earth had I made my daily journey with God so complicated?' I wondered. To live each moment with God would be one of constantly *changing the mind* and *trusting the Lord* (repenting and believing). I now understand that this is the simple (no frills) way to achieve what the Bible calls 'renewing the mind'.

In the 'changing of the mind' one makes a change from one series of thoughts and actions to another; that's fairly obvious. Repentance therefore appeared to be the same, rather like a 'switch', where I could make the switch from going my way to going God's way. I could see that the *being still* and *letting go* were merely the 'tools' to assist me to stay quiet and still on the inside, thus enabling me to turn away from my (ruinous) self-absorption. To trust in Christ therefore, was a positive action, the natural progression to switch from the one to the other.

I'm only stating the obvious here but one must take into consideration the broken-down state of my mind at the time. What was taking place was nothing less than 'Outrageous grace'. To think that the Almighty would go to such

Trust and Obey

'**outrageous**' lengths to win a 'pauper' was quite staggering to me. God had laid it all out before me, in a fashion so simple a fool could understand it. This also is 'Lavish Love'.

Another verse of Scripture came before my eyes: "In quietness and confidence shall be your strength" (Isaiah 30:15). Here in this verse I saw the confirmation. My 'being still' and 'letting go' were providing me with the 'quietness': **my** trust, belief and faith, were providing me with the 'confidence'. "In quietness and confidence shall be your strength," I repeated. That was awesome to me. It was faith in action.

It was even more staggering to me later when I looked up that verse in the Amplified Bible; it reads like this: "In returning [to me] and resting [in me] you shall be saved; in quietness and in [trusting] confidence shall be your strength". (Isaiah 30:15 The Amplified Bible).

Wow! It was all there. I had always thought that 'believe' and 'trust' were lesser activities compared to 'faith'. I thought that faith was the highest of the three. How wrong could I have been? Later I discovered that in New Testament Greek there is but one word used for each. That word is 'pistis' (the verb is 'pistevo' but they have the same root). When in the Gospels Jesus said: "Believe," He used the word 'pistis'. When He said: "Trust Me," He used the word 'pistis'. When He said: "Where is your 'faith'?" or when He talked about the 'faith' that could move mountains, or when He saw their 'faith', He used the word 'pistis'. They were all one and the same thing.

In the Spirit-filled Life Bible, the Bible that I use, the definition of 'pistis' appears in the margin relating to the English word '**faith**' which is highlighted in the Bible text: "have **faith** in God" (Mark 11:22). The quotation is itself taken from Strong's 1,000,000 word profiles and reads as follows: "**11:22 Faith**, *pistis*: Strong's #4102; Conviction, confidence, trust, belief, reliance, trustworthiness, and persuasion. In the

NT setting, pistis is the divinely implanted principle of inward confidence, assurance, trust and reliance in God and all that he says. The word 'Pistis' sometimes denotes the object or content of belief (Acts 6:7; 14:22; Gal. 1:23) (page 1492)."

I did not have this definition of 'pistis' (faith) at the time. I discovered it several weeks later; I only had the definition given in the text of Mark 1:15 of the Amplified Bible which the Lord had shown me in these visions. Nevertheless it was sufficient for me. From where I was sitting as the vision unfolded before me, 'faith' was nowhere near as frightening or even as far away as I once saw it to be.

"Lord," I said, "You are amazing. Why couldn't I see this before?"

"What about '**doing the Word**' and making 'doing' a constant in your life? Constantly hear the still small voice of the Spirit within. Believe... and then do it."

I sat there open-mouthed and then I saw the verse from James that said: "But be doers of the word and not hearers only, deceiving yourselves," (James 1:22). "For as the body without the spirit is dead, so faith without works is dead also" (James 2:26).

I was awestruck; I was floundering in my daily life but now before me there lay five simple steps within easy reach that I could prove moment by moment. Then the Scripture came: "... work out your own salvation with fear and trembling" (Philippians 2:12).

Now, another word I was scared of was **obedience**. The reason being I was trapped in the web of alcoholism, fantasy and pornography; these without doubt came under the category of 'disobedience'. I could see no obedience in my life. 'If I were to be obedient, I could walk away from that stuff, couldn't I?' At least that was my train of thought. But I couldn't walk away; I was trapped and in bondage.

Therefore, disobedience was all I could see. As a result I felt lost and greatly afraid. This was my state of mind. However, at that instant in the vision I saw it: "Doing is obedience!" I exclaimed. The Lord nodded and smiled.

"Oh boy, what a dummy I've been!" I could have danced but I didn't. A moment of decorum seized me; I didn't want to miss anything He said, for all the words He spoke were words of wisdom that dropped like honey from his lips, bringing healing to my broken mind.

I could see it at last. The obedience God required was in each moment. It was not in the past. I had to confess that which was past. In other words, take 'ownership' of my failure, repent (change my mind) and unruffled move on.

Then I saw the words of Paul: "... forgetting those things which are behind and reaching forward to those things which are ahead" (Philippians 3:13). Forgetting those things which were behind was nothing less than *letting go*. 'That was interesting!' I thought to myself. When I did something well, I would rehearse it and relive it over and over in my head and I could live off that experience for days. 'NO!' I could do this no longer; I had to forget those things that were past and reach out for what was ahead in each moment. At that point I noticed that the thing I was feeding upon became foul; it was in fact stale bread. You cannot live off a past experience, no matter how great that experience; you can only live, really LIVE, in each moment.

The obedience that God required was not in the future — two hours time, later today or maybe tomorrow. I had a great tendency to look forward to things and try to enjoy them before they happened. When the moment of fulfilment arrived, they 'disappointed' and 'failed to deliver' simply because they were based upon unreality and because they hadn't turned out the

CHAPTER NINE

way I had envisaged.

Then I saw the words of Jesus: "Do not worry about tomorrow, for tomorrow will worry about its own things. Sufficient for the day is its own trouble" (Matthew 6:34). The obedience that God required of me was in the NOW. Because of my mentality I had the tendency to look to the future and even look to personal prophecy in an unhealthy fashion. I knew that God wanted me to cease from this sort of behaviour and *let it go*. Everything was reining me in, drawing me back to 'the moment', back to *being still* and *letting go* of the future and trusting God in the now — for the now.

Then the Lord said something that shook me rigid once more. "When these five things come together perfectly you will be 'walking in the Spirit'. You will be 'abiding in me' and you will enter into 'the rest of the Lord', for all three add up pretty much to the same thing."

"Hey!" I replied. "I've never made a connection such as that before."

These were three things I'd longed for. I understood their importance and recognised their worth; however, they appeared abstract to me and I considered them to be impossible to achieve. After all, no one had ever taught me how I might attain to such a walk. For example: I've heard people preach on the necessity of abiding in Christ, but I've never heard anyone teach how to do it.

As I thought through those five things: being still, letting go, changing the mind (repenting), trusting and obeying, I began to comprehend the truth of what Jesus was saying to me. It was truly breathtaking to see that "Walk in the Spirit and you shall not fulfil the lust of the flesh" (Galatians 5:16) was something within reach. To 'abide in Me and I in you' (John 15:4) was within touching distance; so was 'he that has entered His rest has himself also ceased from his own works as God did from His' (Hebrews 4:10). It all made me melt away and every pain or ache in my heart to cease. Be that as it may, I could never say that I had achieved these things, because they were moment by moment things. One had to do it, live it, breathe it and stay there, this moment and the next. One could slip from it at any time and that knowledge made me tread carefully. 'So,' I thought, 'that's where repentance (change of mind) and trust comes in.'

"Let us therefore be diligent to enter that rest" (Hebrews 4:11) was the watchword. This is how I saw it: to be 'diligent' was to 'work' those five steps: be still, let go, change your mind, trust and obey. Oh! No words could describe the feeling of relief! I no longer had to strive — all I now needed to do was 'let go' and sink into God.

"I've come to answer your prayer," the Lord said.

"Hey! What prayer?" I was not prepared for what I saw next. In a vision within the vision as it were, I could see myself walking with my dog along the escarpment near my home. "Oh! No!" I exclaimed. This event was during my depression (perhaps 1999) when I was almost at the point of breakdown, consumed by guilt, shame and desperation with no visible way out, at the end of myself. There I was walking along that escarpment crying my eyes out and pouring my heart out to God.

I began to cry once more as I relived that moment and the prayer I'd prayed that day with my dog at my side. I turned and gazed into the loving eyes of Jesus and sobbed uncontrollably; I knew what was coming next!

This was the prayer I prayed: "That I may know Him and the power of His resurrection, and the fellowship of His sufferings, being conformed to His death, if by any means, I may attain to the resurrection of the dead" (Philippians 3:10-11). I used those words of the Apostle Paul as my prayer, and boy,

CHAPTER NINE

did I mean it!

I could feel once more the raw emotion, the genuine desperation, the pain and the ache that I'd felt inside, the sighs and the violence of my crying and the reality of those words as I'd first prayed them.

"I've come to answer your prayer," the Lord said again.

The scary thing — maybe scary is too weak a word — that went through my mind were the other words I'd prayed as I walked along that escarpment. Things like: "I don't care what I have to go through to get it" or "I can face anything if I have You." I would never have thought — not in a million years — that I'd almost have to lose my mind in order to get it!! I've heard many people say over the years: "Be careful what you pray because the Lord answers prayer." Those thoughts went through my mind; but as they did the Lord spoke again:

"Does it matter?" He said to me. "Does it really matter in the grand scheme of things?"

I had no answer. I thought for a moment and then said, "No. It doesn't really matter; You are with me."

He had at that moment given me the mandate for my life in those five steps. I had to be obedient to this Heavenly vision and put those steps into practice.

So it was in this simplified, piece-by-piece, idiot-proof fashion, the Lord unveiled truths that reshaped my thinking and in turn began to transform my entire life. I had always been the type of person who needed to see the blueprint, the working model, to understand the mechanics of a thing. It amazed me to think that is just what He showed me.

As I have said before, everything inside me was manic beyond words; it was obvious I needed desperately to slow down. I don't use the word 'desperately' to overstate, nor do I use it to exaggerate; I use it because I **was** genuinely desperate. I was frantically looking for a way out; here it was within my grasp and it rocked my world.

Who would teach someone manic and out of control to slow down and be 'still'? Whoever would teach a depressive to begin the process of 'changing the mind'? Who, may I ask, would instruct the anxious to 'let go' and moment by moment put their trust in Jesus Christ? An enlightened trained counsellor might, but I certainly hadn't heard this teaching from any pulpit or from any Minister in the Church. Perhaps it was taught, but if so it was veiled to me and I hadn't picked it up. Yet the facts were plain — these teachings were Biblical: they were Truth, and as such they began to set me free.

These principles set me on a journey where I was more conscious of 'dying to self' than I had ever been, more conscious of God than I had ever been, more conscious of the Spirit within than I had ever been and more conscious of the frailty of my own humanity. It took the Son of God himself to spell it out to me, piece by piece, which leaves me awestruck every time I think about it.

The Prayer that Changed My Life

10

The Prayer of Quiet

>Come; be still in the presence of God
>And gaze upon the Son of Love
>You need not say a single word
>For every thought by Him is heard
>The Son of Love is waiting there
>So take some time to sit and stare
>And on Him cast your every care
>You need not breathe a word.
>
>*Rob Giles 2010*

It is fitting that I should now spend some time sharing with you the 'prayer' that changed my life. I wish I could bring to you a book of eloquent prayers, covering every aspect and every angle for breaking addictions (probably to satisfy my own pride) — but I can't. I don't have any. In fact there were times in my journey when I wondered if what I was doing was really prayer at all. Words were not on the agenda. I could not have strung words together to formulate prayers anyway — and God did not require them. I just 'turned up', sat in the presence of God and waited in silence.

"... for silence has a great deal to do with experiencing the Lord on a deeper plane." (Jeanne Guyon, *Experiencing the Depths of Jesus Christ*, p. 93).

I very soon discovered that prayer is **far more than words**. Prayer is an **attitude** of heart; a **connection** with the Father producing **intimacy**.

By waiting in the presence of God, I was simply putting myself in the place where God could work and I was opening myself up for Him to do whatever He needed to do. I had tried to do this all my Christian life and had failed miserably. Yet in the end it was so simple, a child could have done it. Wait a moment — didn't Jesus say something about this? (Matthew 18:3).

Throughout this narrative I have called my way of prayer, 'the prayer of quiet', due to its similarity to that of the 14th – 17th Century Christian mystics. These writers spoke of the 'prayer of quiet'. Jeanne Guyon called it: "The prayer of silence." (Jeanne Guyon, *Experiencing the Depths of Jesus Christ*, p. 93)

I was utterly amazed that I was already doing something similar. The similarity was remarkable (which was more by chance than by deliberation). Now I have purposely used the word 'similar' because there was no yardstick with which to compare what I was doing with that of the Christian mystics. I certainly had no way of knowing whether I was 'doing it' correctly. For that reason I have at times, throughout this account, called it 'my prayer of quiet'. Nevertheless, I did take on board some of the advice they gave as I pursued the Lord Jesus in **my** own prayer of quiet. Their advice did help me to put my attitude of heart into perspective and to formulate this way of prayer. Finding God in a fresh and living way had begun to turn my life around even though I was still struggling with alcohol.

I may be wrong in this, but it is my view that we have to find our own way of praying in this fashion. We must do it in a way that works mutually, for us and for God, but within the

CHAPTER TEN

basic framework. Certain rules apply for this way of prayer to work. The life objectives and attitude of heart are:
    a) to gaze upon the beauty of Christ,
    b) to give Him our love,
    c) to die to self, and
    d) to abandon ourselves to God.

This is a tough call, but it has to be done. We are talking here about breaking serious satanic bondage. There can be no complacency.

As I see it, this prayer breaks down neatly into eight parts, most of which are common and fundamental to that of the Christian mystics. What drives this prayer is our attitude of heart; but it doesn't happen overnight. Our attitude of heart has to be cultivated. It develops as we grow and as we persist in this way of praying. This is my definition of the prayer of quiet: turn up to pray; sit still with the lights off; bring no requests; focus all your being upon Christ; try not to deviate or allow your mind to wander; and hold on to as little of 'self' as possible; receiving everything that happens as being the will of God, and be **thankful.**

Turn up to pray. I use the words 'turn up' because that is what the Lord had told me to do. Simply, 'turn up'. The first thing I noticed about 'turning up' is that it was in my own hands. It was up to me whether I turned up or not. There are no compulsions with this prayer routine. Secondly, there is no expectancy in this prayer. One is not expecting answers to prayer nor is one expecting a miracle; neither does one expect to receive anything. All of these things are set aside in order to meet solely with Christ and to gaze upon Him.

"But when the believer fixes his attention on the face of his Lord without requiring consideration, reasoning, and without needs of proofs to be convinced of anything, this is a higher prayer." (*The Spiritual Guide* by Michael Molinos, p. 5.)

Prayer requests are not the objective in this prayer, just as prayer requests are not the objective in adoration or praise. Thirdly, due to the fact that expectancy is set aside, it no longer matters if anything takes place or not during this prayer. Often nothing will appear to happen while waiting on God; if that is the case, it doesn't matter. All that God wants is for us to 'turn up' and to meet with Him. I have heard it said from the pulpit, "We often seek God for things but rarely do we seek God just for Himself." This prayer method answers that statement.

Sit still with the lights off. To 'sit still' is vital; 'with the lights off' is optional. To be still, and to calm the storm inside is not easy. You may be shocked by that statement and wondering 'what storm?!' Try to sit still and focus on Christ for a few minutes, and you will discover there is a storm inside and, boy, oh boy, what a storm there is. If you don't believe me, try it for yourself. You only have to attempt this prayer for a few moments to see that. To sit still and be still for five minutes in prayer without requests is in fact a tall order. We do not seem to be 'wired' in this fashion in the Western World. Many cannot stand silence.

Without request. To pray and not ask God for things feels strange at first because everything within cries out that we must say something, pray something, or ask for something; but no, we seek for nothing except Him.

"... some people have heard the term 'the prayer of silence' and have concluded that the role the soul is to play in this prayer is one of dullness, deadness and inactivity. This, of course, is not the case. As a matter of fact, the soul plays a higher, more extensive role than in spoken prayer." (Jeanne Guyon, *Experiencing the Depths of Jesus Christ*, p. 93). By making requests, we are satisfying our own need and praying for our **own** benefit. To sit still and say nothing, we fulfil God's need. Does God need anything from us?! You may well ask! I think

CHAPTER TEN

so. When God says words like this: '... let me see your face, let me hear your voice' (Song of Solomon 2:14), it reveals to us His great longing. So, when we sit still and say nothing, our prayer (lack of words but communion of the heart), is essentially for His benefit and not for ours. There are wonderful repercussions to be savoured for our benefit, yet we do not set out with ourselves in mind; we set out with God in mind; not for our pleasure but for His pleasure. Do we have time to give to God alone and listen?!!

To focus all of our being upon Christ. The whole purpose and aim of this prayer is to focus on Christ. He is the object of the prayer and the aim is to gaze upon His beauty. However, we do not see the Lord's beauty with the natural eyes; we see with our spirit. Psalm 27:4 says; "One thing I have desired of the Lord, that will I seek; that I may dwell in the house of the Lord all the days of my life, to behold the beauty of the Lord, and to inquire in His temple." That is one awesome prospect but one that is very much achievable through this prayer. But we must attempt to focus all of our being, that is: our mind, our will, our thoughts, our bodies, our soul and our spirit upon God.

Try not to deviate or allow your mind to wander. Try and keep focus for just one minute and the mind will most certainly begin to wander and you will very soon discover how hard it is to 'sit still', 'let go' and focus upon Christ. This is a stone of stumbling and is the reason why so many who attempt to pray in this fashion give up. One must persist and persevere with this 'prayer'. As we become aware that our mind is wandering, we must stop and resume focus. This will undoubtedly have to be done frequently and may well become tedious. However, what is being achieved in all of this apparently worthless exercise is life-changing and dynamic, although we are not aware of it at the time. It is my belief that this 'prayer', above all else, will achieve submission and surrender to God in our

lives. It will 'quicken' faith and it will open the door to prophetic vision and revelation. This is an awesome prospect.
Holding on to as little of 'self' as possible. To strive to do this is crucial to this type of prayer. Self is a hindrance, a deceiver, and also burdensome.
Self as a 'hindrance': 1 Peter 3:7 shows us how selfish motives and behaviour can 'hinder' our prayers.
Self as a 'deceiver': Galatians 6:3 says, "For if anyone thinks himself to be something, when he is nothing, he deceives himself."
Self as very 'burdensome': I have at times discarded the word of the Spirit through misunderstanding what He had said. Other times I have not even recognised that it was the voice of the Spirit of God who was speaking to me. On both counts, 'self' got in the way and as a consequence I missed it. I have spent almost forty years (at the time of writing) in the wilderness in terms of intimacy with God and I have gone round in circles many, many times in the process. This is the very burdensome nature of self.
Receive everything that happens as being the will of God.
This is another stone that many Christians stumble over. My advice is this: use this stone as a stepping-stone into God. Job did this when his wife said to him: "Curse God and die." (Job 2:9). Part of Job's reply to his wife was this: "Shall we indeed accept good from God, and shall we not accept adversity?" (Job 2:10). Job didn't stumble at what had taken place in his life. He accepted the adversity as being the will of God for him, although it was heart-breaking and a very, very painful experience (the understatement of the millennia). By so doing he was declaring that his life was given totally into the hands of God and that he was resting secure in Him. Nothing and no one would shake him. This is the way in which to use adversity as a stepping-stone: Accept the good as from the hand of God and

CHAPTER TEN

rejoice. Accept adversity as from the hand of God and **learn**.
Be thankful. The Apostle Paul says in 1 Thessalonians 5:17 & 18. "Pray without ceasing; in everything give thanks; for this is the will of God in Christ Jesus for you." Being thankful **in everything** is a very great discipline and it is also the will of God for us. Giving thanks **in** everything is one thing, but to give thanks **for** all things is something totally different. Many Christians would object to the latter; but listen to what Ephesians 5:20 has to say: "Giving thanks always **for** all things to God the Father in the name of our Lord Jesus Christ." Giving thanks to God **for** all things reveals souls that are at total peace with themselves and with God; it reveals souls who are in total surrender and subjection to the will of God and it reveals souls who are content with their lot. As human beings we can very easily become forgetful. We can forget to give thanks even for the good things, particularly if good things take place one after the other as they sometimes do. We can also give thanks for the big things but neglect the small things; we can give thanks for the good and not the bad. I think here of the words of Job, "The Lord gave and the Lord has taken away; blessed be the name of the Lord." I am aware there are believers who struggle and would baulk at this, but let me put it this way: By giving thanks to God we are giving no credence to the devil. So, my friend, don't give Satan any acknowledgement. By giving thanks to God we strike a blow against the evil one.

These eight facets of my approach to God in this type of prayer were powerful. By embracing them, growing in them, walking in them, steadfast and undeterred and making them the 'rules' for my prayer, those same principles gradually became the 'rules' for my life. I personally needed **rules** to give order and structure to my otherwise manic and chaotic mind and my out-of-control life. This approach gave me the order and structure I desperately needed and furnished me with the equipment to 'walk upon my high hills' (Habakkuk 3: 17-19).

Those who walk the hills of Scotland, Snowdonia and the Lake District need the right equipment to do so successfully, skilfully and safely. I also needed to be equipped, and these eight facets of approach to God did just that. By embracing them we embark upon a journey to lose everything (of self), but by so doing we will gain Christ and by gaining Christ we, in turn, gain everything. Such is the paradox of the "Kingdom of Heaven" that is revealed in us.

This then is the ethic of the 'prayer' I adopted. The things I've just mentioned only came to light the more I embraced the prayer of quiet and the more I pressed into God. The waiting on God, the letting go (of the wrong things in my life the Holy Spirit revealed to me) and the 'pressing in' with steadfast perseverance and persistence (in spite of obstacles), brought to pass a gradual undoing of selfish motives, rather like the unravelling of a twisted, knotted ball of string. This statement may appear arrogant but it is not. It is true. It started an amazing journey, but one never arrives at the destination because there is no yardstick with which to gauge one's progress (if progress is what takes place). Nevertheless, there was a shift within me, a noticeable shift, a slow moving-away process — and that was very surprising indeed.

Operating in the *prayer of quiet* is all about laying things down, setting things aside, letting go, giving our stuff to God and releasing our hold; this is nothing less than surrender; but it is all done at the bidding of the Lord Jesus and as He requires. One must **not** go digging around for things to release to Him. This is also very difficult because one would like to hasten the process along, but we must not. It is much like a butterfly struggling to get out of the chrysalis; one must not try to assist it or we shall damage the butterfly. We have to trust that God knows what He is doing. The work is God's so we must allow Him to do it His way and in His time.

At this point I was tempted to abandon all other forms of prayer in favour of this one, because the rate of personal growth was phenomenal. Irritating people were less troublesome to me. I was able to accept people as they were, rather than moan about their faults. My reaction to mishaps too had changed. I sought a solution, a way through instead of grumbling, ceaselessly worrying or flying into a rage. I would now think nothing of the arrival of an unexpected bill, I'd simply say to myself: 'God has not been taken by surprise,' and then trust Him for the outcome. When I had no work I'd thank God and think; 'He has something else for me to do today or else I'm in need of a rest.' After three months of persistent waiting on God one hour per day I was 'pinching myself' to see if I really was alive!! I hadn't gone out of my way to achieve such changes. They had taken place, as it were, automatically. I can only conclude that these things were brought about as a result of opening myself up to God.

The mystics say the *prayer of quiet* is the highest form of prayer, and I agree with them, but only inasmuch as persistent waiting on God will lead a person out of themselves and into intimacy with Christ. In that regard, it is the highest. In my opinion nothing is higher than such intimate communion with Christ. But one must never abandon all other forms of prayer. The Apostle Paul says; "Therefore I exhort that supplications, prayers, intercessions, and giving of thanks be made for all men." (1 Tim 2:1). **All** kinds and types of prayer are valid and acceptable before God, and each has its place and purpose — even to the recital of prayers from a book. I've mentioned the use of written prayers because there was a time in my experience when I would have pooh-poohed such a practice in favour of spontaneity in prayer.

I do have to confess that after adopting the *prayer of quiet* for several months it became increasingly difficult to pray corporately or in public. It was as though I was shut up and words could not be found to pray out loud, yet it was wonderful to hear the verbalised prayers of others; I cannot recall ever recognising their beauty before. I do remember once hearing the still small voice of the Lord saying to me as I listened to their prayers: "Take my hand and walk with me through the candlesticks, cup your hands like a bowl to catch the prayers like incense and offer them to God." As He said those words to me I saw those who were praying as if they were 'candlesticks' bearing a living flame and Jesus walking amongst them to receive their prayers. His invitation to me to join Him was an amazing moment. It was such a beautiful picture of partaking in the prayers of others that my "Amen" just rolled out and seemed so real. Sometimes when it gets tedious in corporate prayer, I think of that picture and the words the Lord spoke to me and my attitude changes.

I have already said that often nothing would happen in the *prayer of quiet*. Or maybe I should re-phrase that statement by saying "nothing *appeared* to happen" and that is true. On other occasions, waiting on God would lead into revelatory vision, or the Lord Jesus Himself would visit me, or angels would come and minister to me. As I persisted with the practice, I noticed that I was becoming far quieter and more still than I used to be. At the same time I was much more alert and watchful and able to let things go far more easily than ever I could before. I was getting to the place where I felt I could not live without this 'prayer'. So for me, from that time onward, waiting on God became a priority and the prayer of quiet was the prayer I adopted.

After a few months I began to review my life. As I looked back over those months I could see what the 'prayer of quiet'

CHAPTER TEN

had achieved in my life and in my business; it was, to sum it up in one word — contentment. The quietness was now permeating my whole being and the business was firmly in God's hands. I was beginning to soar. The Scriptures tell us: "Those who wait on the Lord shall renew their strength; they shall mount up with wings as eagles; they shall run and not be weary; they shall walk and not faint." (Isaiah 40:31).

11

The Secret Place

> Close the door and come on in
> Come on in and sit with Him
> Sit and gaze upon His face
> There within the 'Secret Place'
>
> *Rob Giles 2010*

When we wait on God, as in the prayer of quiet, that place deep down within ourselves where we discover Christ becomes what Psalm 91:1 calls the 'secret place'. "He who dwells in the secret place of the Most High shall abide under the shadow of the Almighty." This verse reveals to us the extraordinary possibility of abiding under the shadow of Almighty God, and such an expectation is much closer to hand than one might think.

To abide under the shadow of the Almighty we must first of all learn to dwell in the 'secret place', which is the place of quiet or attitude of heart where we touch Christ when we wait on the Most High. This is the secret place. The more one waits on God and remains still, the more one discovers the feasibility of being able to stay there (in that state of stillness) and yet to carry it (God's presence) with us into the rest of our day; this is what I would call 'serenity'. One can leave the place of prayer but still remain in the secret place. The spin-off of learning to dwell in the secret place is, of course, that we shall indeed abide

CHAPTER ELEVEN

under the shadow of the Almighty. This, my dear friend, is an amazing prospect.

The place that we choose to meet with God plays an important role but it does not become the 'secret place' (it does while we are there but it ceases to be when we leave). There are two reasons, as I see it, why the place we choose is important. Firstly, it is important inasmuch as we are obeying the words of Jesus, and secondly it is important in order that we learn to shut everything else out (Matt. 6:6).

I think it's more for our benefit than for God's benefit that Jesus suggested to us a place. "But you, when you pray, go into your room" (Matthew 6:6). Jesus knew that **we** needed a place. He knew that **we** needed a time to set aside. He also knew that **we** desperately needed to be able to shut everything out. And finally, He knew that **we** needed to start somewhere.

These are the words of Jesus: "Go into your room and when you have shut the door, pray to your Father who is in the 'secret place'; and your Father who sees in secret will reward you openly." (Matthew 6:6).

Pray to your Father who is in the 'secret place'. I have already suggested that the 'room' is not the secret place. The secret place is our heart and the prayer that issues from our connection with the Father. However, the room is important because there we learn to shut everything out and that is what the prayer in the 'secret place' is all about. It is learning to shut out everything else and to be locked into God.

Sometimes, however, a room may not be physically possible. That should not deter us. The story has often been told of a busy mother with a large family who lived in a small cottage. She entered her 'secret place' by sitting in her kitchen and placing a towel over her head. This was her way of 'closing the door' and shutting everything out. The children accepted this arrangement and respected the fact that she was praying.

Often the secret place for Jesus was to get away on a mountain 'alone' to pray to His Father. Wherever we are, 'alone', with the Father — that is the secret place.

I don't think that 'secret place' prayer is meant for the public arena; it is meant only for the ears of the Father **in secret**; which is why Jesus exhorted us to close the door (Matthew 6:6). There is corporate prayer, and there is prayer in the secret place and we must not confuse the two. I believe there is a definite distinction.

It is my view that we must make sure that this type of prayer stays in the 'secret place'. Intercessors, because of their zeal for God and their zeal for the spiritual, have sometimes been guilty of bringing 'secret place' prayer into the normal church service. Consequently much of the congregation have thought them to be out of their minds, being unable to understand some of the strange goings-on. In the secret place you can weep and wail, roll on the floor, chant and shout to your heart's content and spill out all of your heart's secrets. No one will ever criticise you there or think that you are deluded and out of your mind. (The angels may even join in the ruckus!)

Let's look again at Psalm 27: 4 & 5: "One thing I have desired of the Lord, that will I seek; that I may dwell in the house of the Lord all the days of my life, to behold the beauty of the Lord, and to inquire in His temple. For in the time of trouble He shall hide me in his pavilion; in the **secret place** of His tabernacle He shall hide me; He shall set me high upon a rock."

There are seven key words revealed in this passage about the 'secret place'. It is helpful to dwell a little longer on each.
• **Desire.** We must first of all possess a desire and a longing to

CHAPTER ELEVEN

know God in a deeper way.
- **Seek.** As we continue to wait on God day by day and not give up, we are pursuing God and seeking Him as though He were a very great prize. It is absolutely true that He will become a 'great prize' to us as we continue daily to 'wait' (in the prayer of quiet) and our love for God will grow deeper and richer as a result. It is easily lost, however. When we cease to pursue or press in, it slowly slips away from us. We are so very, very fickle and our love can and does grow cold very rapidly.
- **Dwell.** When we discover God in the 'secret place' we must then learn to dwell there.
- **Behold.** To "behold" or "gaze upon" the beauty of the Lord is the whole object of the prayer of quiet and to fall in love with God. To **gaze upon** the beauty of the Lord is the first aspect of prayer in the secret place and for this we do not need words; we simply **gaze**. It is tragic that we know much about verbalised prayer but appear to know very little regarding 'gazing'. In my opinion, prayer in the secret place is the singular thing that will change our lives and deepen and make richer our love for God. Such love for God is crucial. The more our love for Him develops, the easier it will become for us to walk in obedience. "If you love me, keep my commandments," Jesus said. (John 14:15).
- **Enquire.** To enquire in His temple is the second aspect of prayer in the secret place. This is where verbalised prayer comes into play. But where is the **temple**? Do we have to wait to get to church before we can enquire in His temple? Certainly not!! Paul says that our bodies are the temples of the Holy Spirit 1 Corinthians 6: 19) and it is from within (from the heart) that we make prayers, supplications and intercessions, and giving of thanks (1 Timothy 2:1) and so we enquire in His temple.

- **Hide.** If we are able to discover the 'secret place' and then learn to dwell there, we have this amazing promise: "In time of trouble He shall 'hide' me in His pavilion; in the secret place of His tabernacle He shall hide me." Whilst we are not hidden from the troubles and adversities of life, we can be truly hidden from their harm. Often when we look back over a trial it can feel as though we had been cocooned or hemmed in. That 'secret place' becomes our sanctuary. As we can read in the book of Proverbs: "The name of the Lord is a **strong tower;** the righteous run to it and are safe." (Proverbs 18:10)
- **Set.** "He shall set me high upon a rock." 'Set' is a great word because it gives the impression of being fixed and secure. We are not placed upon a rock from where we may possibly be moved; on the contrary we are 'set' high upon the 'rock' which is Christ. When we began our journey of discovery within the 'secret place' our hearts may well have come from a place of brokenness. We may have been very insecure, fearful and doubtful. As we continue to wait daily upon God and press into communion with Him, there may appear to be very little immediate change 'in the natural', but deep down inside there will most definitely be a growing stability in God. The reason for this is that He has set us high upon an eternal rock.

There is a passage in the Song of Solomon that also confirms many of these things and again reveals to us the two distinct aspects of prayer in the 'secret place'; it is found in chapter 2:14. "O my dove, in the clefts of the rock, in the secret places of the cliff, let me see your face, let me hear your voice; for your voice is sweet and your face is lovely."

Some people who don't attend church and even churchgoers, it has to be said, may be unwilling to accept that the love expressed in the Song of Solomon can also refer to

CHAPTER ELEVEN

God's relationship with us. However, the love of God for human beings is immense, and it is expressed and reflected in the fact that Jesus laid down His life for us. God cannot love **less** than those He created, nor can He love **less** than those for whom Christ died.

Please don't lose sight of the naked truth that I was a broken man with addictions and a messed-up mind. I had no direction and the powers of human reasoning appeared to be out of my reach. This is not **my** teaching — it is from the Lord Himself.

As was often the case during the period of visitation, the Lord Jesus was standing no more than three feet away from me when He conveyed this message to me. With every sentence that He brought to me came wave after wave of love. **Love**, so tangible I could almost reach out and take hold of it. The 'secret place' along with the 'prayer of quiet' was actually laying a foundation in my life. Prayer was central. It played a pivotal role in my journey to freedom and was like a sponge enabling me to absorb **grace** and **love** from God vital for deliverance.

"O my dove", are words of tenderness as from a lover. Such is the love of God to us and for us. "In the clefts of the rock" — there is a line from a great hymn that sums it all up: "Rock of Ages, cleft for me; let me hide myself in thee". That phrase also reminds me of Moses being placed in the cleft of the rock and God covering him with His hand as His glory passed by... he was truly hidden. "In the secret places of the cliff"; these words confirm to us that God is able to hide us in His protective love.

The two aspects of prayer in the secret place are these:
a) let me see your face; b) let me hear your voice.

It is worth repeating that "Let me see your face" is the first aspect of prayer in the secret place. This is where we gaze upon

God and God gazes upon us. This does not mean that God never usually looks upon us; on the contrary, His eyes are always upon us. From our point of view, however, there is a certain term of endearment and great blessing associated with God looking upon us, as the Psalmist says in several places: "Cause His face to shine upon us." (Psalms 31:16, 67:1 & 80:3). From God's point of view, however, He is longing for us to take the all-important step of 'waiting on Him', doing nothing but listening and gazing upon Him in awe. He in turn will gaze upon us. This, dear friend, is the intimacy that many of us are so longing for; it is also the intimacy that God longs from us.

"Let me hear your voice" is the second aspect of prayer in the secret place. This reveals to us that God longs to hear your voice in prayer. It is where we bring our requests, our supplications and our intercessions before God. God is longing to hear us pray prayers that issue from the heart and from the Holy Spirit. As the Apostle Paul says, "For we do not know what to pray for as we ought, but the Spirit Himself makes intercession for us with groanings that cannot be uttered." (Rom. 8:26). When we pray prayers that issue from the Holy Spirit, we will discover prayers that we have never ever dreamt of, (not in our wildest dreams) coming from our mouths, flowing from our hearts and flashing through our minds. BUT they will not be from us, they will issue from the third person of the Godhead, the Holy Spirit Himself. This is the wonder of the secret place. When we close the door and pray to our Father in secret, Jesus promised: "Your Father who sees in secret will reward you openly". (Matthew 6:6). There will be a great sense of expectancy that God will answer our prayers. Revelation too will come to us in the secret place. That revelation will be helpful to others.

CHAPTER ELEVEN

"Let me see your face, let me hear your voice; for your voice is sweet and your face is lovely." (Song of Solomon 2:14). The fact that God so desires to see our face and to hear our voice is almost too much to take in and then to follow it up by complimenting us on the sweetness of our voice and the loveliness of our face is altogether too wonderful for words.

I used to have great difficulty with Scripture of this nature. I thought that God could never love me like that. I knew what I was really like. I could see the mess that my heart was in. If God saw me and knew me this way, I thought He could never love me. This was my way of thinking and my reasoning; how wrong could I have been!

The fact is: God loves us just as we are. The reason for that is grace. Our lives **must** surely change but the simple fact is we do not have to change in order to 'gain' His love. God loved us long before we ever thought of Him, and long before we ever thought of change. "We love Him because He 'first' loved us." (1 John 4:19) and as the Apostle Paul said: "Whilst we were still sinners Christ died for us". (Rom. 5:8).

God is calling us, my friend, into the secret place and to allow Him, as the Scripture says, to "let Him see your face". Can we give Him time for nothing else, except to gaze upon Him and allow Him to gaze upon us? When we do, however, God 'appears' to be utterly 'blown away' with our beauty (Song of Solomon 3:5). Now I have deliberately chosen to use the colloquial phrase 'blown away' because that is how it *appeared to me* from the Song of Solomon 3: 5, which reads: "You have ravished my heart, my sister, my spouse; you have ravished my heart with one look of your eyes." There is always a definitive message of certainty and finality that God wants to convey to us whenever He repeats Himself. "You have ravished my heart. You have ravished my heart". Definitive; certain; final; it is mind-boggling to think that we, mere mortals, could ravish the heart of God! My mind cannot fully grasp that concept. But, since He repeated Himself it seems to me that He must be nothing less than 'blown away'!

At the beginning of this chapter I made a statement: "The more one waits on God and is still, the more one will discover the feasibility of being able to stay there (in the secret place) and to carry it through into the rest of the day. One can leave the place of prayer but still remain in the secret place."

To be able to carry secret place ministry through into our day is a beautiful, quiet and gentle thing. There is no edge to it and there is no 'glory-seeking' in it. It is simply remaining in that place of communion. And Jesus showed us how it is done in Matthew 6: "Take heed that you do not do your charitable deeds before men to be seen by them." The Christian life is about generosity and giving, not just money, but time and energy and even giving of ourselves. Jesus concluded His discourse on charitable giving by saying: "But when you do a charitable deed, do not let your left hand know what your right hand is doing ... and your Father who sees in **secret** will reward you openly," (Matthew 6:3&4). This is secret place ministry carried over into our everyday life. Lovingly and generously 'giving' in secret; our only reward is the approval of the Father, witnessed in our hearts.

Jesus also spoke about fasting in the same passage and warned us not to make a song and dance about it. Jesus said: "But you, when you fast, anoint your head and wash your face, so you do not appear to men to be fasting, but to your Father who is in the **secret place** and your Father who sees in secret will reward you openly." This is what it means to carry secret place ministry into our day, and it is very liberating.

It means that we can pray and fast through our work and everyday living. It means that we can get on with living the

CHAPTER ELEVEN

Christian life, fleshing out Christ in giving and in generosity — quietly, peacefully, gently, lovingly and without ostentation. It means we do not have to be 'noticed' any more, get 'recognition' any more or get 'appreciation' any more (from people around us) for we are noticed, recognised and appreciated by God. This is liberating. What a great burden is lifted off us! Our Father sees and nothing escapes Him. He will reward us openly — but we may have to be in the secret place or at least be 'quiet' in order to spot His 'open' reward.

12

The Turnaround Prayer

> Can you pray for someone else?
> And set your own hurt on the shelf?
> Use your trauma as a stepping stone
> Praying for the hurting soul
> And on your heart carry them home
> By laying down yourself
>
> *Rob Giles 2010*

It was during my thirteen months of struggle with alcohol (the period from the first visitation to when I took my last drink) that the Lord opened up to me the possibility of entering into a further realm of prayer, so simple and so close to hand that it was in all respects rather staggering. I'm not saying that it was a new way of praying, for it was not; it was, however, new to me and quite profound, as many of the things of true simplicity really are.

On one occasion when the Lord Jesus came to me in a vision during the early hours of one morning, He said, "You can always turn things around by praying for someone else." He said this in answer to my probing question: "I'm struggling so much with the drink and the fantasies from time to time. Why am I still struggling so much?" When He made that statement of turning things around, I was stunned and speechless. He then repeated Himself: "You can always turn things

CHAPTER TWELVE

around by praying for others."

Then He gave an explanation which for me turned things completely on their head. "By using your own struggle, suffering or pain as a stepping-stone, you can use it as a point of association in order to identify or empathise with someone and so pray for them instead of praying for yourself. Scripture says, '... knowing that the same sufferings are being experienced by your brotherhood in the world'. By praying this way you will be helping yourself."

The verse or part verse of Scripture the Lord quoted in His statement is found in a short passage in 1 Peter: "Be sober; be vigilant; because your adversary, the devil, walks about like a roaring lion, seeking whom he may devour. Resist him, steadfast in the faith, knowing that the same sufferings are experienced by your brotherhood in the world." (1 Peter 5:8 & 9).

In my mind as I watched, I saw unfolding before me the many ways I reacted during a struggle, a trial, a time of pain or a season of suffering (mainly bemoaning my state and 'poor me' kind of prayers). Simultaneously I heard, possibly for the first time, what that passage of Scripture from 1 Peter ("... knowing that the same sufferings are being experienced by your brotherhood in the world") was actually saying. The penny had dropped!

It startled me for a moment to realise that my Christian brothers and sisters were also suffering the same things as me. I'd been so blind! As a human being I had a tendency to think that I suffered on my own, and that no one's suffering was quite like my own, until of course I watched the news and saw a child with tubes coming out of its jaundiced body and its distraught parents appealing for a kidney. I'd then go off on a 'guilt-trip' because I could not identify with their suffering and didn't know how to pray for them. My prayer then became nothing more than an 'apology' to God. "I'm sorry, I don't know how to pray for these people, Lord;" I'd pray. Those thoughts were like a kick in the gut to me.

I saw also the inappropriateness of comparing my own suffering with that of others or trying to compare someone else's suffering with that of my own in order to empathise; it just doesn't work. It is not good to compare one with another because it takes the effective edge off our prayers and the majority of our prayer becomes nothing more than an apology.

Things went whizzing around in my head as I considered what the Lord had laid before me in terms of this extraordinary way of praying. A line of a Matt Redman song came to mind: "Though there's pain in the offering, blessed be Your name." 'What an offering of prayer!' I thought to myself. I'd often felt unable to identify fully or empathise with someone when praying for them. The thought of being able to use something so simple, and so close to hand as my own pain or my own suffering in order to pray with empathy, was truly amazing. I'd never heard or seen anything quite like this before.

Then some of the mechanics of this type of prayer began to unfold before me. For instance, I saw that if I was anxious I could offer a prayer for those who were anxious or carry a prayer for the anxious on my heart for the duration of my own anxiety. I looked around at family, friends and church members to see potential areas of anxiety and so pray for them. I very soon discovered that my own anxiety attack did not last very long at all, neither was it as powerful as it could have been. The sting had been taken out of it. I was aware that what was taking place was a shift of focus. I was shifting the focus off myself onto others. "By it you will be helping yourself", the Lord had said in His explanation, and that was true; seeing it working in my own life was truly amazing. The real big 'plus' for me was in the revelation that when praying for others

CHAPTER TWELVE

instead of myself, I was declaring to the powers of darkness, 'I'm O.K. in God!'

This was a major move away from the self-absorption of depression and addiction — and a step towards selfless Christianity. I decided to step into this way of praying and as a result it brought about a very great freedom, a change in my personality and character that surprised me. I became much more stable than ever I was before. However, the most surprising thing was this — I was much more comfortable with who I was, much more secure in God and far more sensitive to others and their needs. Not perfect by any means, but there was a definite shift. To experience such stark changes in one's self in a very short space of time is remarkable. It is also a little scary.

I had several opportunities to put this type of praying into action which led me into a sustained and intense period of intercession. I'm not as comfortable as I was in sharing experiences of this nature because they are 'secret place' experiences and as such they are for the Father's ears alone. Nevertheless, I feel compelled to share an example because I am aware that there are many who need to step out of themselves and turn their attention to others. And there are also many who feel called to intercession but don't know how to get started or go deeper. For them this may be helpful.

I was working on a job near Worcester fitting five doors upstairs in a house. In the afternoon I fell down the stairs and broke my collarbone and chipped the socket of my right shoulder. If anyone has broken their collarbone they will know it is very painful and that the pain lingers for around twelve weeks. I began praying for those with broken bones and decided I would carry them on my heart for the duration of my suffering.

Of course I was tempted to question God, 'Why had this

happened to me?' and again, 'You told me to put on my safety gloves when grinding the corroded bolts to dismantle the fence, so why didn't You warn me now?' Instead, I made a conscious decision not to ask such questions but to press into this 'prayer'.

There was pain in my prayer, but I was no longer comparing my pain with someone else's, neither was I using the pain as a prayer for myself, bemoaning my state, nor even having a poor me 'pity party' prayer time. Laying my woes before God had been my regular pattern in the past. I was now using my suffering as a way into God, a point of association, a means of empathy and identification with the suffering of others and offering my pain and my tears as a prayer to God on their behalf.

The Lord showed me that tears also can be prayers in themselves. No tears for myself — what a complete and utter turnaround! No selfish prayers, no 'poor me's, no self-absorption. 'Wow!' I thought. 'This is powerful stuff.'

There was a sense in which entering upon this prayer was a little scary, for I had no guarantee that what I was doing was the 'right thing'. I hadn't heard any teaching on this way of praying. Each time I prayed in this fashion, it was a genuine step of faith. It was **terrifying** too because I didn't know how far I should go. I had never experienced prayer on this level before. The possibilities of intercession that were opening up before me, the depth (or height) to which one could go, appeared limitless. That was what was terrifying to me. There was no one to whom I could go for advice, for I knew of no others who were **deliberately** walking down this particular road of prayer. (No doubt there were others, but I didn't know who they were or where I could find them.) I did feel alone. I was fearful too, because there appeared to be such a great responsibility, obligation even, the like of which I had not experienced before in prayer. 'Help me Lord not to miss this,' I

CHAPTER TWELVE

prayed because I felt so weak; 'You alone must teach me, for the task before me is so great.' I guess I would not be human if I hadn't held back a little.

I very soon discovered once more that it was not necessary to verbalise prayers. Such prayers could be without words. As the Scripture says; " ... with groanings which cannot be uttered" (Rom. 8:26). I had to 'carry' this burden on my heart for as long as God saw fit; I made that choice very early on. It was all in God's hands and I would allow myself to be carried along by whatever happened.

One morning when I woke early to pray, I began with the prayer of quiet, possibly for around twenty minutes. Then I prayed for the suffering church and for those being beaten as I felt the pain in my shoulder and the uselessness of my right arm. Then as I prayed, in a vision the Lord took me to the prisons and forced labour camps of Eritrea (a small country between Sudan and Ethiopia). I saw (sensed and felt) the squalor and the untold suffering, the merciless beatings and the broken bones. I looked into their eyes and saw the grief and the pain etched across their faces; such imagery I can almost see again as I write. I rolled the floor in agony and sobbed profusely as I cried to God; no words were possible. The burden lifted slightly as I went to work but was still in the background as I carried them on my heart. I breathed out verbal prayers from time to time, shed a few tears, sighed and groaned a little as I worked. When I was in company the burden lifted, but returned when I was alone, sometimes with a power that brought me to the floor and reduced me to tears. This season of intercession lasted for close on two months.

Never before had I experienced a time of intercessory prayer of that nature or magnitude. I would never have considered it possible for me to have prayed in that manner. What's more it all began by simply using my mild suffering and turning it into prayers for others. I noticed two things. First of all, I was no longer comparing my suffering with that of others. Secondly, I was able to continue to do my manual work.

To my utter amazement, I was able to continue fitting doors throughout the twelve weeks of recovery, apart from four days which I had off when I felt I could work no longer. The pain did not go away throughout those twelve weeks, but I was able by God's grace to pray for a people group that I would never have considered praying for, except perhaps fleetingly in a 'suffering church' prayer meeting.

To be able to use my own suffering as a stepping-stone and turn it into a prayer for others was a monumental thing. Each time, however, I had to make a decision whether to 'step into' this prayer or not. Each time it was a definite step of faith. At least that's how it seemed to me, because I hadn't experienced faith on this level before.

When we make a deliberate move to pray for someone else when everything seems to be out of our control, we are declaring our security in God and that we are 'OK' even though we do not feel it. By deliberately refusing to pray for ourselves we are stepping into the security of God and declaring in the face of the devil that our life is in God's hands; we are 'secure' and 'OK' even though we certainly do not feel it. This actually is a step into faith, a step out of ourselves into God; it also encourages faith to develop and grow. It encourages stillness and calm; it encourages surrender to God... Awesome!

Faith, stillness, calm, and surrender to God were things that could not be found in my life when I was depressed; they were stifled and shut out because I had become self-absorbed. I was not aware of it at the time but looking back, I see that it was true in my case. The pain, the trial and the problem were the dominant issues for me in my depression, and I needed to turn

CHAPTER TWELVE

these things around. By praying in the fashion I have described I wasn't denying my pain, my trial and the problem I was facing, but I was taking steps not to allow those things to **rule**, **dominate** or **crush** me!

Three things were taking place here: a) I was planting my feet in the footsteps of Jesus. Our Lord prayed for those who crucified Him (Luke 23:34). b) By praying this way I was resisting the devil. As we read in 1 Peter 5:8: "Be sober; be vigilant; because your adversary, the devil, walks about like a roaring lion, seeking whom he may devour. Resist him, steadfast in the faith, knowing that the same sufferings are experienced by your brotherhood in the world." In this scenario, I was resisting the devil not by shouting and screaming at him and trying to take authority over him, but by simply ignoring him... Nothing infuriates the devil more than ignoring him and giving him no credence. c) When I prayed this way I was entrusting my trial and its outcome to God.

When we pray for someone out of our own pain, despair and anguish, refusing to pray for ourselves, we are making a monumental shift towards placing everything into the hands of God. This is dynamite.

In a vision the Lord said something that surprised me. "When you act and pray in this manner, you are entering into my suffering." For me these were awesome words. Even to contemplate the possibility of entering the sufferings of Christ was something I believed to be reserved for the likes of the Apostle Paul or Mother Teresa and completely out of reach to the 'average' Christian like myself. It seemed to me to be a saintly mystery that was unattainable. Awestruck, I began to think once more of the time I poured out my heart to God as I walked the escarpment by my home with my dog at my side. I thought once more of those words of Paul, "That I might know Him and the power of His resurrection and **the fellowship of**

His sufferings."

When I saw those last five words I exclaimed out loud, "You're kidding me!"

"No, not at all," the Lord replied. "This is the fellowship of my suffering when you fellowship with others in their suffering."

Some words of the Apostle Paul that I'd never understood went through my mind: "I bear in my body the marks of the Lord" (Gal. 6:17) and, "And fill up in my flesh what is lacking in the afflictions of Christ" (Colossians 1:24). These Scriptures were a step too far for me and although I cannot claim to understand them, I certainly saw them in a different light. Just the thought of being able to enter the suffering of Christ, however, was almost too much to take in.

To be able to use one's own suffering as a stepping-stone and turn it into prayer for others is a beautiful thing. I've said this before but it is worth repeating. Each time one has to decide whether or not to 'step into it', each time it is an act of faith.

Facing the Truth ... to Make Way for God

13

Back to the Start (a visionary reflection)

> Sometimes it's good to sit with God
> And there with Him connect
> Whilst sitting there alone with Him
> Give worship and respect
> He may show me things I should have done
> But I try not to object;
> He may take you where it all began
> As you sit there and reflect.
>
> *Rob Giles 2010*

I had now embarked upon a journey from which there was no turning back. I suppose I could have gone back if I really wanted to. But I was aware that it would have been a major act of rebellion on my part to have done so. I was somehow 'cocooned', 'encapsulated', and surrounded by God; however, at the time I was genuinely unaware of it. It's only now, as I look back, that I see how 'kept' or 'held' I really was through that period.

The revelatory visions I have described in previous chapters all took place within a few weeks of the first visitation. A lot happened in a very short space of time. I had a deep conviction

Back to the Start (a visionary reflection)

now that what I was looking for lay within easy reach. My journey of 'prayer' was in its infancy (and still is). I was learning. But somehow, I sensed that God was saying to my heart, this learning process would continue throughout my life — that dented my pride somewhat. I don't think I was quite expecting something of that order.

During the subsequent visitations and visions there was much teaching, equipping and dare I say... being 'taken apart' by God — piece by piece. The teaching that the Lord Jesus brought to me answered many puzzling questions. It also formed the basis of the message that God was calling me to share. I wanted to tell the world **now**, this minute — but God wouldn't let me. As I 'waited on God' it became clear that the Lord didn't want me just to share theories, but He wanted me to share real-life answers to everyday questions of faith and Godliness — answers that were **proven** in my own life. He was calling me to **prove** them for myself in living them out **before** taking the message to others. I've often heard this statement and it is perfectly true: "You cannot take anyone where you haven't gone yourself".

So for the time being, I had to 'work through' whatever the Lord showed me. I had to live it, breathe it and make it a part of my life. I had to keep pressing into God through the 'prayer of quiet' and walking in each aspect of prayer as the Lord Jesus had taught me in the Heavenly visions. I had embarked upon a journey with Christ and I did not want to go back.

A day or so after the revelatory vision regarding 'trust and obey', the Lord Jesus came to me again while I was praying. After reflecting on some of the things He had shown me I said: "Lord, you are so amazing; I never imagined I'd ever see things like this." Then as He had spoken in previous encounters, His words were as though He had tossed a grenade into my thinking; bringing me up with a start and shattering my

CHAPTER THIRTEEN

immediate train of thought.
"You could have had this in 1971."
"Hey!" I exclaimed, shocked and rocked. And then in the presence of the Lord I began to think back to where it all started, back to my early days of youth, of 1968 to 1971, and to reflect.

Maureen and I had met in late September of 1968. We were married the same month of the following year and rented a little house for 35 shillings a week. I was an apprentice engineer and still at college at the time.

My friends and a few work colleagues were on the fringes of the drug culture; two of them were dealing. Our little house became a centre where we all gathered together to smoke pot and listen to the music of Frank Zappa, Captain Beefheart, Jimi Hendrix, Pink Floyd, Black Sabbath, Deep Purple and Led Zeppelin. My friends began to experiment with mandrax, amphetamines and LSD and two of them subsequently went down the heroin trail. Somehow, miraculously, Maureen and I didn't go any deeper than to smoke pot.

Some of my associates (but I don't know who) raided a chemist's shop and the stash of drugs was hidden in our garden. Around the same time on the way home from a T. Rex concert in Birmingham, we were pulled over by the police. It was about two o'clock in the morning and the rain was bucketing down. There was a group of about eight or ten of us in the back of my friend's VW van, my wife included. As we heard the police siren behind us, one of the quick thinkers among us gathered all the drugs that were in our possession and dropped them through a hole in the rotten floor of the van onto the dark, wet, open road. I never did find out if anyone went back to retrieve them. The police were not stupid. They knew we were in possession of drugs but of course they had no proof; they couldn't find them. After the subsequent search they let us go.

Back to the Start (a visionary reflection)

A shop that was situated across the road from our home was broken into and the old lady proprietor was seriously assaulted. None of our group had anything to do with it, I'm glad to say. The police made house-to-house enquiries to find out if anyone had seen or heard anything. Maureen was in the house with our first child when the police arrived. "Is your Mum in?" the police officer said to my wife, not realising that she was the tenant and the mother of the child she was holding in her arms. We hadn't seen or heard anything at all and the police officer's visit was the first we heard of the incident. From what we could gather the old lady had been sprayed in the face with a nasty substance.

The police calling at our home did make us sit up and think, because there was a substantial amount of cannabis in our possession. Thankfully that stash of drugs hidden in the garden had been moved to another location. Had the police been suspicious though, they would easily have discovered the cannabis. My wife and I were very naïve and totally unaware that we were putting our child at risk. I think we were more scared of being caught than anything else. I know I was.

Our home was pretty much an open house. One of my friends was homeless and stayed with us, dossing on the lounge floor. He had a huge record collection which I enjoyed immensely. He spent most of his time smoking dope and tripping out on LSD. One time on LSD he had what he called a 'bad trip' and was smoking marijuana at the same time. He could easily have burned the place down whilst being *non compos mentis* when he dropped the lighted 'joint' and burned a hole in the settee. How the settee didn't catch fire is a mystery — furniture was not particularly fire resistant in those days!

Three Hell's Angels from the Wolverhampton chapter came round one evening and they were soon tripping out on Speed. Late into the night and into the small hours of the

CHAPTER THIRTEEN

morning the music was playing and we were out on the street with guitars, singing and dancing. One of the Angels was wielding a knife as he danced! It was after that incident we received intelligence that the police were watching our house.

That was the point where my wife began to call time on the fracas, and asked my friend to leave. To put him out was a major step, because he was the guru, the godfather of our group. Maureen was thinking and making decisions for the benefit of our child — something I hadn't considered, since my head was 'somewhere over the rainbow'.

This was the situation out of which both of us came to Christ. In the October of 1970 I completed my apprenticeship and left the company to make my way in the big wide world — and failed miserably. I was becoming a waster. By the July of 1971 I was on my sixth job after either walking out or having been sacked; each time it was "the foreman's fault" (well, that's what I said). At that point we had another child on the way. This work situation was not good and so Maureen was seriously considering leaving me.

I started my new job on Monday, 5th July 1971. The first person I got friendly with was a fellow named Alan Southall, a born-again Christian (that's how some liked to be known in those days). At break-time we ate our breakfast together and he shared the love of God with me. I'd never heard the Gospel message in my whole life before and I don't think I'd ever met a born-again Christian before either. I was intrigued to discover that as a human being I was a sinner and that Christ had taken the punishment for my sin upon himself, as a result of which forgiveness of sin was freely available to me through confession, repentance and faith in Jesus Christ.

Over the next couple of days I questioned Alan relentlessly; I was hungry. I suspect that Alan didn't recognise that it was hunger; I think he thought I was testing him or "taking the

Mick" as he put it. I just drew everything out of him — salvation, redemption, judgement and the Second Coming! On Wednesday 7th July 1971 about two o'clock in the afternoon, I gave my life to Christ standing by the side of my machine reading a tract that Alan had given me. I prayed and meant the sinner's prayer which was printed on the back of that tract. I knew something had happened inside me; instantly I was changed. That was the moment I first believed.

At an appropriate moment I told Alan what had happened. No one had ever come to Christ through his witness before; he'd only ever received the brush-off from those with whom he'd shared his faith. So it was not surprising that he didn't believe me at first. But by the time we were walking out of the factory and on our way home, I had managed somehow to convince him that I had genuinely asked Jesus Christ into my life.

The change was dramatic. I told my wife and she was thinking to herself, 'Oh no, not another fad!' I told all of my friends what I had done. I genuinely wanted to go for everything that was available in Christ; this is perfectly true and I say this hand on heart. A couple of days later Maureen gave her life to Christ, which was to me a great relief; we could now go on together. Next day on the Saturday, I was baptised and by the 12th July I had received the baptism of the Holy Spirit.

There was a gentleman who was a member of the church Maureen and I began to attend, whose name was Mr Watts. There was something about this man's spirit that drew me to him. He wasn't a preacher and he never did anything as one might say 'up front'. He did however spend much time privately in prayer. He also made cards and wrote in them a message of encouragement and sent them to people. Maureen and I received two such cards and messages. He and his wife would turn up for the occasional service, when he was feeling

CHAPTER THIRTEEN

well enough. This brother was terminally ill; yet he was so peaceful, so at rest and content with himself. I recall asking him what his secret was, because I genuinely wanted what he had. A short while later he gave me a little booklet which he said gave him a great deal of comfort when he was in pain. Much of the contents of this little booklet were taken from the book by Brother Lawrence called 'The Practice of the Presence of God'. This was his secret, believing that he was living in the presence of God moment by moment. Shortly after giving me the booklet, he passed away from this world into the arms of Jesus Christ.

I had tried to put into practice what the booklet prescribed but I found it difficult. The main stumbling blocks were my own feelings. I couldn't 'feel' that I was in the presence of God. But nowhere did the Bible say that you had to 'feel' that you were in the presence of God to actually be there; it was a faith thing. But that hadn't registered properly. There was always a lurking doubt at the back of my mind, the thought that the Lord might desert me or that He could not presence Himself with me because I was so bad. Of course the truth of the matter is that living in the presence of God is not based upon our feelings; it is, as I have already said, based upon faith. I knew it in my head but I could not translate that element of truth to my heart.

Oh, how I wish I'd stuck with that little booklet and persevered! Practising His presence would no doubt have saved me a great deal of heartache, sorrow and pain. I don't mean that it would have kept me from trouble, hardship or suffering. A Christian is not exempt from these things and we are foolish if we think so. But I do believe that it might not have been necessary for me to have had a mental breakdown or even have had to wait a further 33 years in order to experience the 'stillness', 'quietness' and 'rest' that 'abiding' in His

Back to the Start (a visionary reflection)

presence undoubtedly brings.

Now, one must remember, at this point, that the 'reflection' I have been describing took place in a vision and the Lord Jesus himself was standing to one side, a little to my right, no more than three feet away. I turned and looked at Him because I was 'gob-smacked'. I didn't say anything — I just stared at Him open-mouthed; but the question was in my heart and I somehow knew that He had read what I was thinking. He didn't answer verbally; He just looked at me and smiled as if He was confirming my thoughts. I knew that this experience of 'rest' and of 'peace' in the presence of God was part of what He meant when He spoke those searching words to me: "You could have had this in 1971".

I recalled also that back in those early days of my Christian life stillness, peace and the presence of God were genuine desires of my heart; I longed for those things. I knew that had I stuck with what that dying brother had given me and had I sought more earnestly to look beyond my feelings, I might well have found what I was looking for. People in various places and at various times over the years have remarked about the gift I have of praying. I hadn't taken it very seriously — I was looking for something more, always for something more. What a fool I'd been! It was there within my reach all the time, crying out to me: "Here I am; take me up"... I had to repent.

Also in those early days as a Christian in the summer of 1971, I witnessed to all and sundry. I was almost fearless in sharing my faith with others. My friends, people in the drug culture, tramps, the poor, the broken; those were the people I felt that God wanted me to reach with His love. They were also the people that many Christians had confirmed to me prophetically as being the ones God was calling me to minister to and reach with the Good News. I was on the brink of something back in those days. Had I practised the presence of

CHAPTER THIRTEEN

God, taken up the call to prayer more seriously and persevered with sharing my faith with others, the ministry that I later longed for would no doubt have flowed quite naturally. Instead it had been like trying to grasp the wind or taking hold of water and trying to stop it from flowing through my fingers.

I'd thrown it all away. It was fear of man, wrong thinking and wrong choices that had led me to 'desertion'. Every time I preached the Gospel or witnessed to anyone it was a battle and I had to momentarily wrestle with myself before I could seize the opportunity. What a fool I'd been. For the truth is that sharing the love of God with someone is not easy at all. Every time it was a challenge: sometimes I'd get it right and sometimes I'd get it wrong. But I gave up and withdrew from the field. I deserted.

I could take you to the exact spot in the very street where, like a fool, I said these words; "I'm not going to witness like this any more." From that moment something died within; it was as if my witness was put on hold and I became crippled within. Over the years which followed that foolhardy moment, I tried to convince myself that my calling was to the Church and not to the lost, broken and dying. I sought after ministry, I longed for ministry, but I can honestly say I never found complete fulfilment or total satisfaction in whatever I did, nor did I enjoy God in the way I could or should have done. I had walked away from my primary calling. When I saw this I had no option but to confess (own it) and repent.

The people I was reaching in 1971 were the very people God had called me to. When I stood in front of the congregation at the Caribbean funeral I had the confirmation within me that this was my calling. It had been there all along, though **I** had **dismissed** it. Those words: "You could have had this in 1971" cut me to the quick, cut me in two and tore me down.

Back to the Start (a visionary reflection)

"You'll have to break the curse I've put upon myself," I said to the Lord, because in reality that was exactly what I'd done. I'd brought a curse upon myself with my reckless vow of never wishing to witness again. "You'll have to help me to overcome, Lord."

The Lord replied, "When you are through this, tell others and show them the way out. Your life will be a living example."

14

The Mantles

> You say, "This stylish coat of mine
> I want you all to see
> The very many things I do
> Come on and look at me"
> "No, wear this shabby coat," says God,
> "Wear it as your overcoat
> And walk humbly with Me."
>
> *Rob Giles 2010*

One morning I arose around three a.m. and went downstairs to pray. This practice was fast becoming my custom. Not especially getting up at three a.m., but getting up to pray whenever I awoke. There was a sense of great expectation that morning, as though I knew something was about to happen. It was with ease that I began to pray and almost instantly the Lord Jesus was there with me in the vision.

I then reached out to take His hand — a practice I had performed at the commencement of almost every visitation or vision. The one thing that was really wonderful was He never ever objected; He always reciprocated by taking mine. This occasion was no exception. He took my hand in the vision and led me to the place that He had prepared. I say this because it's how the vision unfolded and we conversed there together, face to face.

It was a cold wintry place where He took me and there was a fire of coals between us. I noticed that at His feet there were three 'mantles' lying on the floor. As I looked on He picked up one of them and offered it to me. For a moment I didn't know what to do or what to think, but I reasoned that if I took it, I certainly wasn't being covetous. I wasn't about to take it purely for my own adornment. He'd offered it — so I reached out and took it.

It was plain, simple and unattractive; there was nothing special about the mantle that anyone might desire as a 'must have' item. But I sensed I should put it on. As I slipped it over my head, even before it touched my shoulders, I knew what it was; it was a 'mantle of humility'.

The Lord Jesus gave no treatise, message, description or any pearls of wisdom regarding this mantle except that He gave this piece of advice: "Never take it off," and after a pause He concluded by saying, "Let this be your outer garment; wear it above everything else." There were no great feelings when I put it on, in fact I didn't even know that I was wearing it. All that went through my mind were a few simple thoughts concerning humility that I'd heard preached from the pulpit thirty-odd years ago. Apart from that, there was nothing.

Afterwards, this mantle in itself became a message to me, speaking deeply to my innermost being. This is how it spoke to me: just as there was nothing special about the mantle that anyone might desire as a 'must have' item, in the same way I hadn't desired humility either, nor had I sought to live it out and make it part of my life. I had never sought to take the lower place. I had always wanted to be 'seen' to be spiritual. I wanted to be seen as the man of God. But wait! Wasn't that what the Pharisees had done? I also saw that very many Christians too had not desired humility because it appeared to them to be something that was just not 'cool'. They think

CHAPTER FOURTEEN

mistakenly, as I had, that by seeking humility and taking the lowly state they will lose something or even lose out by it. Many even think that meekness is weakness, which is tragic, because in actual fact, humility is great gain. "For God resists the proud but gives grace to the humble" (James 4:6).

The fact that there were 'no great feelings' when in the vision I put the mantle on, suggested to me that there would be no great feelings associated with walking in genuine humility. In fact humility is one of those things that people who have it, don't even know they've got it. If you think you've got it, the chances are you haven't got it at all, because there's an element of pride associated with the thought: "I'm humble!" Only the people who see the way you live, react, respond and speak, know that you've got it. All that is required is to be lowly of heart. "Wear it above everything else," was the Lord's advice. In other words, let it cover everything else. Let humility be seen, rather than 'how wonderful you are'. I felt that I'd been all too eager to blow my own trumpet, just as the Pharisees had done.

Meanwhile, Jesus was picking up the second mantle and offering it to me. I wasn't prepared for what took place when I put this one on. As I slipped it over my head I again knew instantly what it was; this mantle was a 'mantle of forgiveness'. It was like being struck with a bolt of lightning. Physically it hit me, rocked me and shook me to the very core, and like that flash of lightning so it flashed across my eyes.

When I was fully robed in the mantle of forgiveness I saw, as though in a movie, incidents from my life where I needed either to forgive or else I needed to receive forgiveness from God. I relived each experience. I felt once more the same emotion, hurt, pain or anger that I'd felt when the event had actually taken place — events right from birth through to the present day.

I felt once more the trauma of having the umbilical cord around my neck and I began to cry as I relived the experience, hearing once more the story that my mother and grandmother had often told me, how my life was saved by a bossy midwife. I thanked God for His mercy that I'd flouted. And the Scripture echoed through my mind, "Before I formed you in the womb I knew you, and before you were born I sanctified you and ordained you a prophet to the nations." (Jeremiah 1:5). And I cried again.

I was back at school where I'd written the play. I was crying profusely as I saw the teacher's face before me. I knew I had to forgive her. It was difficult, hard and painful but Jesus said to me: "Let go — forgive — move on." As I forgave, the Lord said again: "Now move on."

Then before me there was another incident where I needed to forgive. As I did so the Lord said again: "Now move on." I faced one at a time, incident after incident and event after event where I needed to forgive. Each time as I forgave, the Lord Jesus said to me: "Now move on." When He said those words, "Move on", it was as though He was saying: "Let go", and as I did so it seemed to trigger the next thing I needed to face — or that He wanted me to face.

When I say that I "faced" these things, I mean that I saw them in the vision and relived the experience. Everything took place within the main body of the vision and in this I was 'encapsulated' with Christ because the vision touched me both physically and emotionally. The word 'encapsulated' describes perfectly how I felt. I was literally engulfed, cocooned and swallowed up in God; I was protected. Although it was a very painful, emotional and heart-rending experience to say the least, it was a **safe** place where I was — a **very safe** place and I knew it. God will not take us through an experience such as this unless it is 'safe' and unless we can take it. God means no

CHAPTER FOURTEEN

harm by it ... and He makes it 'safe' for our healing and freedom. These two mantles He gave me (for I was wearing both), I am sure, provided me with all I needed to forgive and to walk free.

On occasions the situation I saw was one in which I needed forgiveness. On such occasions as these, I had to receive the forgiveness from God and accept the fact that I was forgiven and then I could move on to the next.

As I moved on with the Lord Jesus through this experience, I was sobbing uncontrollably and my body convulsed with emotion. I'll say it again... I relived the grief, the hurt, the pain, the sorrow and the anger that I had felt when the event originally happened. All of the original emotions accompanied the memory. This often takes place in counselling sessions. This was not a counselling session; it was a vision, but the effect was very similar.

There were six particularly traumatic events I had to face and in all of them I needed to receive the forgiveness of God as well as to forgive others. The first was when my Mother died and the indifference that I'd felt. The indifference at her funeral was rooted in the fact that as a six-year-old child I'd felt a twinge of abandonment when my mother remarried and went to live elsewhere, leaving me at my Grandmother's. I'd made it sound as though it was my choice to stay there at my Granma's, but I felt that my Mum didn't 'fight hard' enough to keep me. There was the child's cry within me and I felt it once more, "Mum — Mum! Fight for me — show me you love me!" Oh, the intrigue of our minds!! What foolish games we play!! I couldn't ask for forgiveness, for the Lord wouldn't let me; He'd placed His finger across my lips. I couldn't say a word — I simply had to receive it — nothing more — nothing less. I could have asked for forgiveness until the cows came home and not got anywhere, but forgiveness was **there,** it was **all around**

me. I just had to reach out and take it. This was a difficult lesson to learn, but I didn't have time to pussyfoot around, He was saying to me, "Now move on."

I was crying profusely as I faced the second traumatic event. This was **huge**. I don't think anything could have prepared me for that moment. In the vision I relived the moment when I was sexually abused (repeatedly) as a child. I knew now for the first time (since the event took place) that my abuser was a woman. That was a shock!!! I also knew for the first time that my perverse sexual behaviour was partly rooted in this event. But — I had to **forgive**... for the mantle I was wearing was furnishing me with the grace to do so.

I had kept all of this locked in... and it had 'screwed' me up. As a seven-year-old child my mind had shut down and I had blotted out the horror of those events. I now had to forgive myself for that. I had no time to argue with God or with myself because His grace and power were in me and all around me, urging me forward. God was in me — God was all around me — God had forgiven — and I had forgiven! Then I heard the Lord say, "Now move on." My ribs at that point ached as though I'd taken a beating because of the violence of my crying.

The third traumatic event I faced in that vision was when my Grandmother died. I didn't shed a tear... her passing meant nothing to me... even though she was the one who had brought me up and had given me everything. This was awful! She was the one person who had really loved me and in return I'd loved so much as a child. How could I have possibly been so hard and callous? This puzzled me, but I had no option but to repent and receive the forgiveness of God. Later I discovered the reason. You see I'd felt that she had let me down when I was abused. She hadn't done anything wrong and she probably didn't even know that it had happened. It was, however, a

CHAPTER FOURTEEN

child's cry in the dark; "Gran, why didn't you save me?!" "Where were you when I needed you?" Then again the Lord said, "Now move on." I was crying rivers of tears at that point.

Then shock — horror! ... I was face to face with the guy who had sexually abused me as a teenager. I could remember every moment of that event and I loathed it and I **loathed him** (I've emboldened those words to express the intensity of how I felt) and now I had to forgive!! ... I stuttered a little in doing it (perhaps a lot) ... but I did it. I forgave — and I forgave from the heart.

Then in the vision I faced my wife and our former pastor. I had long thought they'd **robbed** me of ministry and I had held it against them. To come face to face with this was also difficult and painful — and I was ashamed. It was indeed a result of my own misunderstanding as much as my own obsessive longing for ministry. However, I had to forgive, let it go and move on as He had told me; and so I **forgave**. My difficulty though, was not particularly in forgiving but it was in the 'letting go'. For a brief period I had to wrestle to let the thing go. Whenever the 'robbery' came to mind, I had to let it go, otherwise to have held on would have destroyed my peace and eaten me away as a canker. I had been touched by the 'destroyer' already — far too much in fact to allow this thing to take root and become a root of bitterness. I could not face that kind of 'muck' again.

Finally, I faced those with whom I had worked (or had been employed by) in the period leading up to and during the breakdown. The 'blame game' surely had to cease. I could not carry grudges any longer; I had to let go — and forgive.

There were many unanswered questions hanging over what they had done and indeed what had happened to me in that place of employment. Of course there are always many unanswered questions surrounding such circumstances. By internalising such questions, I knew that I would be undoing what God was seeking to achieve in my heart and that was to bring healing. I had to *let go* of those questions and feelings and refuse to allow myself to be engulfed or swallowed up by asking the whys and wherefores. This was not easy but Christ was calling me to walk with Him in each 'moment' and to trust Him. Although I couldn't fully understand what was happening to me, I knew I had to forgive and to forgive from the heart.

The power of the risen Christ was furnishing me with the resources to forgive and even to protect and shield me from harm. These mantles of humility and forgiveness were but symbols of that. What must be borne in mind is this: it is always a **safe place** in the presence of God — He will always shield and protect us from damage. So I forgave... I forgave... I forgave. The whole experience turned out to be the best therapy I could **ever** have undergone.

I was at this point lying physically on the floor — like a wet rag — all cried out. I could not have shed another tear even if someone had paid me or even if my whole life depended upon it. My eyes were so sore that I could barely see; my ribs ached as though I'd taken a beating, but something had happened! There was within me a deep sense of joy, peace, release and liberation; this was for me the beginning of freedom.

This mantle of forgiveness, like the mantle of humility, was also to be worn continuously. The exact words that Jesus said to me were: "Never take it off, wear it next to your skin, and let it become a part of who you are." I love that phrase, "Wear it next to your skin". What a great privilege to live and breathe forgiveness! What a very great freedom!

Somehow I knew that to walk in forgiveness was possible to achieve. It could be accomplished by being still and watching, then additionally by letting go and by the changing of

CHAPTER FOURTEEN

the mind, all of which boiled down to repentance, trust and obedience. 'To walk in forgiveness — wow — that truly would be a daunting prospect!' I thought to myself. But somehow or other I felt that it was within reach; I was now ready for it.

I staggered to my feet. Between us (that is, between the Lord Jesus and myself) was the fire of coals exactly as it was before. The one remaining mantle was lying on the floor at His feet. Somehow I knew that this mantle represented the ministry to which God was calling me.

This third mantle was multi-coloured, suggesting to me a multi-faceted ministry. However, they were not bright summer colours but rather dull, autumnal colours — mainly greens, browns and yellows. This in turn gave the impression that the indicative ministry would not be so 'up front' and 'in your face' but more peaceful and sedate — more earthy and relational. Perhaps I would be ministering to people who were in the 'autumn' of their trials and be able to lead them through the 'winter' into the spring!

The ministry was first and foremost that of prayer; I knew this in every fibre of my being and I trembled. All the other aspects of life and ministry I sensed would stem from, and flow out of, the prayer and intercession just as the greens, browns and yellows seemed to come out of the main colour of the mantle itself. The main colour was difficult to distinguish. As the light caught the material, so it appeared to change colour. When I thought it was one colour it changed to another. Perhaps the chameleon-like nature of the mantle indicated the many aspects to prayer and the many types of prayer. Perhaps it also indicated that I could be 'all things to all men'... I could only speculate.

God was calling me to unusual prayer and I knew it. The task appeared to me to be so great and almost beyond my reach, so much so, that I wanted to scream: "No!" and run away and hide. I was trembling, anxious and even frightened, as the Lord picked it up and offered it to me. I didn't want to take it at first... At last I plucked up courage and reached out to take it. To my surprise, He walked around me and draped it over my shoulders.

As He did so I became very much aware of two things. Firstly, I hadn't taken this mantle to myself because it was something that I'd desired or that I had craved for; He had given it to me of His own free will. Secondly, I hadn't even put the thing on myself; He'd put it upon me. This was powerful, very powerful, for it revealed to me beyond any shadow of doubt that this was indeed His will and a 'call' to me from God.

I thought this mantle would be heavy, very heavy. However, as the Lord put it over my shoulders to my surprise it was just the opposite. It was light, very light and with it came the words: "My yoke is easy and My burden is light." (Matthew 11:30).

I was surrounded by light. "God, You are amazing!" I exclaimed and I began to dance. I danced right out of the vision and around my living room, through the hallway and into the kitchen. I praised God and praised God over and over again. I became aware that the soreness of my eyes from the crying **had gone!** Gone also was the **aching** of my ribs! This was the first time ever in the whole of my life that I'd felt **yoked** to the Lord — truly yoked to the Lord — and I danced, praised and gave thanks some more. I made an attempt to share with Maureen what had taken place and then it was time for me to go to work. I say that I "made an attempt" to share with Maureen, because how in the world could I share 'this' — and do it justice?!

15

A Bizarre Encounter

> God may turn you upside down
> Or turn you inside out
> Sometimes His work is too bizarre
> For you to figure out
> Dear friend you have to trust Him
> You know that He knows best
> God has a way to turn things round
> So that you will be blessed.
>
> *Rob Giles 2010*

It was several weeks later that I had four doors to fit upstairs in a house for a customer. I guessed it would be a hard day because the house was old and I had noticed the door frames were somewhat out of shape when I'd gone round to measure up a week or so earlier.

I was alone in the house, as the occupier had to go out. As I worked, a strange encounter with God took place. His presence was all around me and I became alive inside with the Holy Spirit. I was 'overshadowed by the Almighty'; I think that was what was happening to me.

Brief communications relating to my five 'companions': 'be still', 'let go', 'change your mind' (as an act of repentance), 'trust' and 'obey' were being transmitted to my mind by the Holy Spirit of God. They were being expounded to me in a similar fashion to that of a sermon. Things such as: 'Entering the rest of God', 'Abiding in Christ' and 'Walking in the Spirit' were topics that came out of the message. (These, you may recall, were the three things that the Lord had said would take place when the 'five' came together perfectly.) Other things such as: 'Living a Life Surrendered to God', 'Suffering as a Christian' and several other prophetic messages were also expounded to me during the course of that day. In truth, the Lord did not label any of the messages during the exposition. The titles I chose later in an attempt to process what was spoken to my heart and to my mind. After all, I was in that house for eight hours and in my estimation I'd heard around six hours of Holy Spirit-induced sermon. That was an awful lot to digest and an awful lot to process!

I was in a complete daze. Work-wise, I hadn't a clue what I was doing; I was operating on auto-pilot (almost unconsciously if that is possible) whilst at the same time being aware that the Lord was at my side and that His presence was all around me. And yet, I was insensible to what I was doing and to what was going on around me 'in the natural'. The prophetic exegesis **from the Lord** was the like of which I had never heard preached!

Running through my mind concurrently with this 'exposition' — I don't know what else to call it — were meditations on the five key things Jesus had revealed to me in the visitations, namely: be still, let go, change your mind, trust and obey (I can't get away from them). These five wove in and out of the message the Lord was speaking to my heart, and my meditations (or the Holy Spirit's meditations) flowed naturally and seamlessly into (and out of) the Lord's message. The reality of this is very difficult to convey. It's all very much impossible... naturally speaking. One would need to be a mental gymnast.

CHAPTER FIFTEEN

As He spoke this message to me, He would often break off for a moment, to tell me what to do regarding my job in hand (for, as I have said, I hadn't a clue what I was doing). I was lost in this 'exposition', while at the same time hearing the instructions He gave and following them through without any hesitation or question, robot-fashion. The bizarre thing was, these instructions He gave were accurate and very precise.

For instance, while holding a door against the frame to see what needed to be done, He said something like this, "Take a quarter of an inch off the bottom and taper the top a quarter of an inch from the nose." (The 'nose' being the top corner of the door, latch side). I set off to do it, while all the time He continued with this awesome exposition. Then out of the blue, "Mind the light," He interjected. I stopped and looked up to negotiate the lightshade on the landing as I carried the door downstairs to the garage where I was to perform the cutting.

When the necessity arose for machining, each time the Lord would tell me what tool to use and direct me in its handling. Once in a stupor I staggered into the garage with a door. "Lay the door on the benches," He said to me. "Take the circular saw, set the stop for three eighths of an inch and use it on the bottom edge of the door." All the time His 'prophetic message' was being transmitted to me.

What must be borne in mind here is that this was the job I did every day, the job I loved and the job I knew inside out; I didn't need to be told what to do. But I surely did on this occasion! If God desires to get through to us, He can make us into a dummy or a buffoon for a moment in order to get our attention but get our attention He will. I've often considered the madness of Nebuchadnezzar when he ate straw like an ox (Daniel 4) whenever I think about this incident!!

I recollect often while using the electric plane that He'd tell me when to stop. If I stopped too soon He'd tell me to take another pass or maybe two passes. Each time the instructions He gave were absolutely spot on, so that the door could be fitted accurately.

Once as I came downstairs carrying a door, there was a cable lying across my path which I didn't see. "Watch the cable." I stood motionless and tried to gaze down at the floor; there at my feet was the cable. Stepping over it, I proceeded to walk to the garage, thanking God as I went. I surely would have tripped over that slightly raised cable. I'd neither seen it, nor could I see it, because my vision was impaired by my tears.

Such were the extravagant occurrences of briefing (regarding my work) the Lord gave to me that day, along with His exposition and 'my' or the Holy Spirit's meditations, all running simultaneously, it makes me blink rapidly when I think about it. It's enough to make you 'flip your lid' as I put it, yet at the time it all seemed so natural.

There were during the course of the day, other more personal, private and intimate prophetic communications that the Holy Spirit spoke to my heart. These were regarding my life first and foremost and later regarding my family, my work and my ministry. However, it would be inappropriate or unseemly to disclose their content, other than to describe the effect His searching eye and prophetic message had upon me, in order to convey the bizarre nature of this encounter.

I have remarked earlier, how to my surprise the Lord did not mention my sins or perverse behaviour when He first visited me. Instead He empathised with my pain and heartache to win me with 'Lavish Love'.

He showed me the seat of my problems — my mind — and how I might change my thinking, conduct and demeanour. However, it is true that at some stage in our journey we must surely face up to our sins, our demons, our hurts and hang-ups if we are truly going to walk in the freedom that Christ brings.

CHAPTER FIFTEEN

We cannot escape that, unless of course, we have been nurtured in the Christian faith all our life, and have therefore allowed the Lord to deal with our sins at appropriate points, so that there is only minimum pain.

This was one of those times. In fact this was now the third time where I had to face my own rubbish, impediments, junk, bosh and paraphernalia, whatever you want to call it (sin if you like), and take ownership and responsibility for it. The blame game had to cease; the buck stopped with me. I could no longer say 'he or she made me do it'; 'it's their fault'. If I were to come to you and vomit in your home I would have to take responsibility for my own mess, apologise and clean it up. So it is with this; at some point we surely must take ownership and responsibility for our rubbish.

Without any doubt at all, what I had gone through and the depths to which I had sunk, were my own fault and no one else's. It was my mess. Taking ownership and responsibility for one's own mess is key to recovery. Don't let anyone fool you into thinking otherwise.

The prophetic words He spoke (I use the word 'prophetic' because the words He spoke were living and active) seemed to cut me in two, so that my heart ached and tears streamed down my cheeks dripping onto my shirt or onto the floor. I couldn't see what I was doing or where I was going because of the tears; neither could I think straight or even determine what I was doing, for the message was tearing me apart. His message had done this to me before, albeit for different reasons.

I was in no way, shape or form like the older brother in the Prodigal Son parable, who had always been with the Father and obeyed His wishes. I had squandered my inheritance and virtually thrown it back in the face of God just as the prodigal son had done. I cried rivers of tears; surely my heart would break. Yet God's message of love to my heart was lavish and

His promises extravagant and this was conveyed both within and around me. I did not deserve these things on the basis of my reckless and wanton behaviour.

I had no strength; the weakness was debilitating. Groaning under the burden and power of His word, I sighed, and breathed out cries to the Lord for help. I could hardly put one foot in front of the other, let alone carry the doors up and down stairs. I cried profusely due to the intensity of the Lord's piercing and searching message to my heart and my body convulsed. It seemed madness to proceed with fitting the doors and operating power tools. Be that as it may, there was no escape. He **would not** let me run.

"Trust me," He replied, speaking into my uncertainty and confusion, and then continued with His prophetic discourse, interspersed with the unequivocal instructions. This was the state I was in when the 'cable incident' took place.

Shortly after that occurrence my customer emerged. Instantly the flow of my tears was stayed, the message halted, my strength returned and in my right mind (for the want of a better word) I was able to converse normally with him as though nothing had happened. We chatted together for around ten minutes over a much-welcomed cup of tea.

There was a small mirror on the wall and being a little vain I glanced into it as we talked. I was taken aback; considering the violence of my blubber there were no visible signs that I'd been crying. My customer took his leave and disappeared somewhere, leaving me alone. No sooner had he gone than it all began again: the stupor, the prophetic message, the tears, and as for my strength, well it just got up and deserted me.

When God is chasing us down in order to answer our prayers, nothing will get in His way. He will surely find a way to get our attention; just as the dumb ass spoke to Balaam to stop the madness of the prophet (Numbers 22 and 2 Peter 2:15,16)

CHAPTER FIFTEEN

and as a light brighter than the sun blinded the Apostle Paul on the road to Damascus (Acts 9:3-6). At several stages in our lives we may well have opportunities to face up to our sins, habits, self-righteousness and hypocrisy. The best piece of advice anyone could possibly have is this: "Don't resist when that moment comes."

This bizarre encounter with God opened up a door in my heart to another possibility that left me quite speechless and truly amazed. I considered the way in which I had been sustained during this encounter: my needs had been met and my work did not suffer in any way, shape or form. I considered also that God had called me to prayer and to intercession and I began to put two and two together. If God laid upon me a prayer-burden no matter how heavy, or if He led me into a period of sustained intercession I had these assurances — He would keep me, He would provide for me and my work would not suffer. As I thought through this whole encounter and considered these things, the fear and the anxiety I had in connection with the depth of prayer I was being led into began to leave.

This encounter was also a powerful time of healing and restoration for me although it did take several days to get over the whole experience both physically and emotionally. "Search me, O God, and know my heart; Try me and know myanxieties; and see if there is any wicked way in me, and lead me in the way everlasting." (Psalm 139:23,24) During the events leading up to the breakdown, I was fool enough (or maybe wise enough in hindsight!) to pray those verses and use them in my prayers. No surprises then; God answers prayer!

Such a simple prayer as those verses from Psalm 139 can be so powerful and life-changing; I think that it is important for our own spiritual well-being to pray that prayer from time to time. But we must not try to dig around in our past or search for things ourselves, because it would not be helpful. We must ask God to do the searching and allow Him to show us, in His way and in His time. This is the healthy way of growth.

I had reason to return to those premises several days later and whilst there, I was able to assess my workmanship. I was amazed. Upstairs I had fitted four doors perfectly. The door frames had been so badly distorted (as I pointed out earlier) that it would have taken a great deal of work, time and patience under normal circumstances for me to fit them properly. Yet I had done it virtually blind and without thinking for myself. God was amazing and so good to me. I just gave thanks again and again, with a feeling of deep gratitude for His guidance.

Eternity had collided with my out-of-control, diminutive and puny world and I knew it. It had breached all my defences and broken into the chaos of my mind. Eternity, in the form of Christ the living word (John 1:1 & John 1:14) had collided with me. I'm smiling to myself as I write this; after all I might just as well have collided with a sword! In a way, I had! (Hebrews 4:12)

16

Choices, Growth and Breakthrough

How can you choose when you're blind to the choice?
How can you hear if you can't hear the voice?
You can't really live where there's too much to lose
No growth will there be if there's no power to choose
So choose I say — choose well and grow
For your breakthrough will come
Where your fears cannot go.

Rob Giles, January 2011

After that bizarre encounter I was listening for the voice of God much more than I'd ever done. Yet from time to time I was still overcome by alcohol. On the one hand, I was aware that something dramatic was taking place. I had an awareness of God that I had not experienced since my conversion. The drinking binges too, were far less frequent and certainly not as heavy. On the other hand, however, there was an 'inner pull' drawing me to the drink which I could not resist. It appeared to me that I was overcome so very, very easily. I was in a dilemma and the contradictions threw me into confusion.

This was not a particularly good time for me; it felt as though **all hell** was let loose upon my soul, much of which was undoubtedly of my own making. Nevertheless it was a hellish

Choices, Growth and Breakthrough

time. I concluded that the battering I was taking was all because I had made one simple decision — to give up alcohol. Some say that the turmoil is backlash from the devil because one is running after God. But I chose not to believe that. I chose rather to believe that God was at work, bringing all things to the fore in order to deal with them. This was the way I read the situation...

I thought back to my college days in the Engineering Laboratory, melting lead in a ladle over a Bunsen burner. When the heat was turned up the lumps of lead in the ladle began to melt. The impurities of the molten metal would then rise to the surface forming a layer of what was called 'slag'. This slag could then be skimmed off (with care of course), leaving behind the pure molten metal in the ladle.

God used this analogy through the prophet Zechariah when He said: "I will bring one-third through the fire. I will refine them as silver is refined and test them as gold is tested. They will call on my name, and I will answer them. I will say, 'This is my people,' and each one will say, 'The Lord is my God' (Zechariah 13:9).

The Apostle Peter too in his first letter used the same analogy: "In this you greatly rejoice, though now for a little while, if need be, you have been grieved by various trials, that the genuineness of your faith, being much more precious than gold that perishes, though it is tested by fire, may be found to praise, honour, and glory at the revelation of Jesus Christ" (1 Peter 1:6,7). I chose to believe that this metaphorical refining process was actually taking place through the turmoil I was in.

I have mentioned an 'inner pull' drawing me to the drink, a pull that I could not resist. This irresistible pull is what alcoholics and drug addicts call the 'cravings'. But I don't think, for one moment, that this irresistible inner pull would have been so evident, prominent and pronounced had it not

CHAPTER SIXTEEN

been for sitting and 'waiting' in the presence of God. Everything appeared to be accentuated by 'waiting'. It seemed to me that the cravings intensified, the more I 'waited' and the more I prayed. The more I prayed, the more I discovered things about myself that I'd rather not have known. And that's enough to make anyone give up on 'waiting' and praying in that fashion. Nevertheless, I chose to 'wait' in prayer.

I made the choice because that was what the Lord had told me to do. My reasoning was this: How else would I be convinced of the truth? How else would I know where I stood with God? How else would the Truth of Scripture be translated from mere head-knowledge, to genuine conviction, reality, and faith in my heart? For it is through trials, testing and suffering that Godliness is established in our lives. In his book *The Spiritual Guide*, Michael Molinos writes:
"The inward way is a centring of the whole being in a loving manner in the Divine presence. There the Lord operates! It is by Him that virtue is established; it is by Him that desires are eradicated; it is by Him imperfections are destroyed." (page 64)

I certainly needed a shot of this virtue... Big time! I discerned from the writings of Molinos that it would be a painful journey. If God was really at work eradicating my selfish, sinful and fleshly desires, then it would be a painful rollercoaster ride. If He was at work destroying my imperfections, then the heat would have to be turned up, so to speak. If I were to pass through such a refining process it would doubtless be a painful process. This was my train of thought and as such it became clear to me that it was no time to quit! But it **was** a time to be quiet: "Stand still, and see the salvation of the Lord" (Exodus 14:13).

Self-effort was no longer in my reasoning. I'd had my bellyful of self-effort in trying and losing, trying and losing. If

I fully believed steps 1 & 2 of the Twelve Steps, then I would know beyond any shadow of doubt, that **I** wouldn't be able to see the power of alcoholism broken merely by self-effort!

"Step 1. We admitted we were powerless over alcohol — that our lives had become unmanageable. (*The Twelve Steps — A Spiritual Journey* page 256.) If I truly believed that I was 'powerless', as step one suggested, how then could I possibly think that I was suddenly in a position where I could break free myself?! I could not. How then, after years of trying and failing, could I suddenly believe that I was in control?! How then, could I possibly think that I could manage the 'unmanageable?! It's impossible, it's ludicrous.

"Step 2. We came to believe that a power greater than ourselves could restore us to sanity." (page 256) The 'power greater' than myself, was God. How then could I possibly believe that I could do it myself and restore myself to sanity??!! Yet those who have a dependency perform this act of stupidity all the time. In their heads they know that they can't do it on their own, but foolishly they act as though they can!! I know. I did it all the time! Consequently, I became trapped in that 'vicious cycle' of winning and losing, and going round in circles. This was now time to *let go* and rest in God in silent prayer, **ignore** my storm and win. There appeared to be no middle ground and no sitting on the fence at that stage of my journey. Rightly or wrongly, I chose to believe and to 'wait'.

The way in which I ignored my 'storm' was to pray for others. I used my 'storm' (confusion and emotional disquiet) as a connection, a point of identification, in order to pray for others, as outlined in Chapter 12. Now, it has to be said that I didn't set out with the intention in mind of ignoring the storm. But it soon became evident that that's what I was actually doing. When I became distressed and turned my distress into prayers, the effect was the same as if I'd simply ignored my

CHAPTER SIXTEEN

storm. This approach was not negative like repressing or suppressing one's feelings; **it was positive**. In fact, it was dynamic and action-packed because it often led me into serious periods of intercession.

At such times, when I felt that my world was falling apart, I prayed for those whose world had literally fallen apart. I prayed for those who had lost everything in the floods, earthquakes and other disasters. The sense that my world was falling apart was in fact untrue, nevertheless the feelings I had were very real. By praying in this way, it became far easier for me to overcome the caving-in feeling and to bring my out-of-control emotions under control. I was, in fact, turning my attention away from myself and turning it towards God and towards others. I was ignoring the storm and activating **faith** — the very thing that I had formerly been terrified of! In a matter of a month or two I had developed a genuine concern for others, which surprised me. "Is this real?" I asked myself, "is this really happening to me?"

There were many moments when I felt like singing and dancing — but I refrained. I didn't allow myself the indulgence of getting too excited; I simply **gave thanks** to God. I refused to go over the top, for I had been learning not to be moved by the 'lows'; I also had to learn not to be moved by the 'highs'. To continue to swing between such extremes would not have been helpful at this stage of my journey. I sensed this was what the Holy Spirit was saying to me, and I tried to be obedient. I must confess, that it did feel quite foreign to 'let go' of exuberance. But I felt it had to be done.

I had discovered the hard way that to rejoice too much was unhelpful in my mental state. I had a habit of getting 'locked' into things all too easily. Inevitably, I'd go over the top with exuberance and stay there in a manic state. What would ensue would be a massive emotional 'downer', followed by a drinking binge. To be down and still remain in a manic state of mind is incomprehensible, but that's how I was at that time.

On the other side of the coin, I could get discouraged all too easily. In no time at all I'd be 'lower than a snake's belly', so to speak, depression would set in followed by another drinking binge in order to be manic, and so become what I believed was normal. It was a toss up in any given situation as to which side the coin would fall, whether I'd be high or low, up or down. Either way, I'd still be manic and end up drunk.

Learning to be *still* and to *let go* were vital to **my** mental well-being. These 'two gems', accompanied by the prayer of quiet and what I have termed the turnaround prayer, were leading me to a place of calm, balance, and poise, things I'd **never** known or experienced before, and that was truly remarkable. By cultivating stillness, quiet and prayer, I was developing a sense of rest in God; a sense that, in God, I was truly 'O.K.' I did wonder, at times, whether I had died and gone to Heaven, because the changes that were taking place were in stark contrast to how I'd always been.

The choices and decisions I made may not appear to be tough at all, but they were to me, given my mental and emotional state at that time. There hadn't been such a thing as 'self-control' in my life before, certainly not in the areas I have discussed. Besides, I would not have known how to set such a thing as self-control in motion. In an addictive situation, it is as though commonsense has sprouted wings and flown. To make life-changing decisions, and to take life-changing steps, is almost like tearing yourself apart. For you are, in fact, tearing up what you know and trying to replace it with something that you don't know. You are tearing up your very own blueprint for life; and that is unthinkable. Just the very thought of 'believing', and going beyond my fear, regardless of how I felt, was indeed **terrifying**. The mental and emotional turmoil, the

CHAPTER SIXTEEN

fear, the terror, and the panic attacks associated with the steps of 'faith' were huge. A simple step of faith was like taking one giant leap into a vast chasm called the unknown.

To go beyond that fear, in terms of life-changing decisions, is a major, major step for one who is dependent upon alcohol or drugs. I certainly could not have made any of those choices and decisions had it not been for the Lord Jesus Christ, coming to me and leading me by the hand.

During this stage of my journey I was learning to accept everything that came my way as being from the hand of God. This turned out to be a very shrewd move, because over the next few months I became aware that what I was doing, was in fact, attacking my anxiety and paranoia head-on. For instance, if an unexpected bill came in, ordinarily I would have got myself in a tizzy. I would have worried ceaselessly about where the money would come from and I'd drink to calm my nerves. But, by this simple act of accepting the situation as from the hand of God (letting it go and resting in God), I was actually declaring that I was O.K. and secure. I was allowing myself time to think things through rationally. God had not been taken by surprise and God would provide. Thus, unwittingly, I was declaring my security in God. This was a giant step, believe me, in rising above and breaking out of my locked-in mental state. This one step was simplistic in reasoning and yet so tough in execution, but its consequences were massive and far-reaching. My insecurity had lain rooted in anxiety and paranoia. But now, with anxiety and paranoia largely nullified, I was very soon aware that I was journeying toward a place of rest and contentment in God. Rest and contentment were things I'd never detected in my experience before.

During my thirteen months of struggle to quit the drink (from the first 'visitation' to my last drink), the storm of my 'addictive temptation' raged. It raged inside, outside, and all around me. The ongoing battle with pornography also raged, but I did feel held and cocooned by God. I made several other choices during that period of time. One of these was if, or when, I could finally quit the drink, I'd stay off it — a choice I now believe to be of the utmost importance.

I also made a determined effort to quote positive Scriptures, both out loud and to myself. I also played certain worship CDs relentlessly. Fill your mind with 'good' and you will get good out. Fill your mind with 'garbage' and you will get garbage out. I tried to operate on that principle.

In addition, I began to shut down every avenue of acquisition regarding alcohol and pornography. I wouldn't allow myself to venture into certain pubs and off-licences. Nor would I allow myself to enter certain newsagents and petrol stations. I sought not to glance at the 'top shelf', so I avoided the places with the greatest display. I made the life-changing decision not to have personal access to the Internet, because I felt I couldn't trust myself. In addition I had parental control locks on the Adult T.V. Channels without knowing the password. These were monumental decisions to make and they greatly restricted me. But I felt they had to be done. The Lord had said to me in one of His earlier visitations: "Close the door Rob." I not only had to attempt to close the door on my thoughts but I also had to close the door to every avenue of acquisition.

This of course is impossible without GOD. The best way I found to let these things go was in the prayer of quiet as I waited on God. Isaiah says: "Have you not known? Have you not heard? The everlasting God, the Lord, the Creator of the ends of the earth neither faints nor is weary. His understanding is unsearchable. He gives power to the weak, and to those who have no might He increases strength. Even the youths shall

CHAPTER SIXTEEN

faint and be weary, and the young men shall utterly fall. But those who **wait** on the Lord shall renew their strength; they shall mount up with wings like eagles, they shall run and not be weary, they shall walk and not faint." (Isaiah 40:28-31)

Then came the moment I'd waited for, when finally everything came together and fell into place. It was so ridiculously simple. I had been in a similar scenario to this a thousand times over. But you see... this was now God's moment. When that moment arrives it is but a simple step to freedom.

One day in mid-November 2005 I finished work early; it must have been around two thirty in the afternoon. I sorted a few things out with my supplier in preparation for my work the following day and then set off for home, calling into a pub for a drink on the way. It was probably the only pub I allowed myself to venture into. My normal pattern of drinking at that stage was to have one or two and then go home. Formerly I would have gone home and drunk all night, but not now; things were changing.

I hadn't eaten that day and the drink went straight to my head. As I stood at the bar I suddenly became aware, acutely aware, that I was ogling the barmaid. I was trying to shut down the sexual fantasies at the time and at that precise moment of conflict, I saw possibly for the first time that the drink opened the door to, and also heightened, my sexuality. I thought to myself: 'I don't want this!' So I finished my drink and walked out. And that turned out to be the last time I had a drink. It was God's time, the moment I had longed for and prayed for, where everything fell into place. I believe that such a time cannot be manufactured or self-induced. It certainly was that way for me.

After that moment, I was too scared to take another drink. Too scared of what it might do to me and too scared of where it would take me. I was certainly too scared of having to go through all that 'excreta' again. The word 'excreta' is vile, it is filthy and it is vulgar. To the addict or alcoholic in recovery, that word is a fair description of the vile, filthy, vulgar mess they have been in. It had been a painful journey, a far too painful journey to quit the drink in the first place, let alone having to go through all that agony and 'junk' again if I took that first drink.

I could not at that point testify at the 'Twelve Steps' or other meetings: "**I've** conquered the drink." I thought instead, 'I'll wait and see.' I did this for several reasons. I had been in similar situations many times over, where I had thought that I'd beaten the drink, only to find that it came back with venom to bite me. I'd often thought that I'd beaten it. This time, however, my approach was different. If I was free, then I had to know for certain that it was God alone who had done it. Self-effort was no longer in my reasoning as I have said before. This in itself was an amazing place to be.

I also sensed that my victory was ongoing. I had both to maintain and manage it. Temptation would surely come. The way in which I handled enticement would be the key issue. Words cannot express how important being *still* and *quiet* with God was in the process of maintaining and managing my new-found freedom.

For anyone to break free from an addiction there will undoubtedly be many difficult choices to make. Don't be fooled into thinking otherwise. Looking back over my journey, I believe that one of the greatest decisions I made was if, or when, I could finally quit the drink, I would stay off it. This was nothing less than 'burning my bridges', 'closing the book' and 'turning my back' upon it. There is one thing I have learnt over the last five or six years. To toy with the notion of sitting in the sun, having a nice quiet drink with friends is not going to

CHAPTER SIXTEEN

work. The alcoholic in recovery has to decide: "Once free, stay free". It will take courage, make no mistake about it, but if we have the grit to take one step, God will take two to meet us.

Summing Up

17

Roots

> Many chains are broken
> And the victory almost won
> But the journey is not over...
> It's only just begun.
>
> *Rob Giles 2010*

During the summer of 2005 I had a visionary dream while waiting on God in the early hours of one morning. This vision proved to be very enlightening. I saw two angels digging around a tree in order to remove it from the ground. Coming to a root, they stopped and one of them hacked through it with an axe. The two then resumed digging until they came to another root. Once more the root was hacked through with the axe. For some considerable time, this course of action went on, digging and cutting, digging and cutting, until at last they came to the tap root (a vertically growing root). At that point they were able to lift the tree out of the ground with ease, rather like pulling up a carrot.

I sensed that the meaning of the vision related to my alcoholism and other bondages. God was showing me that there were many things hindering recovery, just as the roots hindered the angels from pulling up the tree. I have listed below several specific hindrances revealed to me through the

CHAPTER SEVENTEEN

vision, where my responses and reactions had been, in reality, the cause of my addiction. I have touched on these things as I encountered them in my journey, but I was unaware of their significance and unable to see how they correlated until the vision. The things I've listed below are by no means exhaustive, but I hope that these scanty revelations will at least cause you to **stop** — **think** — and ask God to show you what is stopping you from breaking your habit.

This is my list of roots:
lies
resentment
triggers
fear
abuse.

These are what I now term "the subconscious 'rules' of addiction". They do not cause the addiction but they do serve to keep us ensnared and unable to get free. I believe that these 'rules' are what we may call 'self deception'. They also reveal to us 'the intrigue of our minds'. As the Scripture says, "The heart is deceitful above all things, and desperately wicked. Who can know it?" (Jeremiah 17:9).

- **Lies:** are the wrong thought processes or un-truths that keep us tied into an addiction or dependency. A lie can have every appearance of truth, even to the point of convincing us, but it is a lie nevertheless.

The first 'lie' I had to confront was denial. *The Twelve Steps — A Spiritual Journey* says of denial:
"Denial is a key survival skill. We protect ourselves by not admitting that anything is wrong. We ignore the real problems by replacing them with a host of elaborate explanations, rationalizations, and distractions such as minimizing, blaming, excusing, generalizing, dodging, attacking, etc." (page 79).

I had been in denial for many years, always skating around

the issue and never admitting that I had a problem. The first step to recovery was when I finally admitted I had a drink problem. It plunged me into darkness because I didn't have the resources to deal with it or to overcome it. Nevertheless, it was the first step to freedom.

As an abuse victim I had also blamed myself. Such apportioning of blame was in fact untrue; it was a lie. In truth, someone had taken advantage of me against my will, and I did not have the strength, courage or the resources to fight back. My belief that I was in some way to blame was nothing but a lie. Jesus said: "And you shall know the truth and the truth shall make you free." (John 8: 32). Therefore to believe a lie or even a half-truth (if there is such a thing), will render us unable to get free. On the other hand, to begin to accept the truth, no matter how painful, will become a giant stride to freedom.

Nearly all of my Christian life I have lived in the realms of my feelings and emotions and they have governed my reactions and responses. And, boy oh boy, have they been hard taskmasters! The way that I **felt** determined whether I was up or down, but of course that was not the truth. Again it was a lie. I'm not saying that feelings and emotions are wrong, nor am I advocating that we should suppress them; certainly not. But to allow our feelings and emotions to govern our thoughts, reactions, and responses, is living in falsehood and it is unhealthy.

If I **felt** unloved, I would **believe** I was unloved. If I could **feel** the presence of God then I would **believe** that the presence of God was with me. If I couldn't **feel** His presence then I would conclude that His presence was not with me. If I had an encounter with God, I would want to **hold on** to it. When I **felt** the reality of that experience slipping away, I'd feel guilty and then begin wondering what I had done wrong to lose it. Such

CHAPTER SEVENTEEN

feelings were untrue and nothing more than **lies**. I gradually came to the conclusion that I could no longer trust my feelings, for they had **lied** to me. I tried, therefore, to look beyond my feelings and to believe the things that were constant and certain in the Scriptures. I repented of each manifest lie in turn, denying myself the luxury of believing that they were true and I placed my trust in God. Jesus said: "If anyone desires to come after me, let him deny himself, take up his cross, and follow me." (Matthew 16:24).

A major part of the '**cross**', that a dependent in recovery has to take up, is the denial of what he or she feels or sees in order to simply **believe**. This kind of self-denial is a massive step towards recovery.

- **Resentment.**

"Resentment is a major roadblock to recovery that must be removed. Resentment is the bitterness and anger we feel toward those whom we perceive as threats to our security or well-being or those who have caused us harm. If not removed, our resentments hinder our progress and growth." (*The Twelve Steps* page 79)..

At this point I think of three common examples of unresolved resentment. They are: to bear a grudge; to harbour bitterness; and to be engulfed by unforgiveness. These three had a destructive impact upon my life. I was so blind and naïve. I hadn't realised that my drinking and other habits had their roots in these three 'devils', but until they were challenged and removed, my recovery from the drink problem would be seriously hampered.

My conclusions are these: bitterness only eats us away. To bear a grudge stems from the feeling that 'we are owed' something by those who have harmed us. This, however, only breeds hatred. Unforgiveness, on the other hand, puts us in a torture chamber.

Joff Day in his book *Forgive, Release and be Free* says: "Another thing that happens is that they try to bury the hurt. Then defence mechanisms build up on the inside, both mentally and emotionally. These negative thought patterns (strongholds) promise to protect a person from getting hurt again. For example, 'I'll never get involved with a woman again.' 'He let me down badly. I'll never do business with his sort again.' Rationally these defences make sense. But that which is built up to defend, quickly becomes a stronghold that imprisons." (page 15.)

In the parable of the unforgiving servant, Jesus said: " 'I forgave you all that debt because you begged me. Should you not also have had compassion on your fellow servant, just as I had pity on you?' And his master was angry, and delivered him to the torturers until he should pay all that was due to him." (Matthew 18:32-34). The story of the unforgiving servant only serves to reinforce what actually takes place in reality.

Are we tortured if we do not forgive? Oh yes! You bet your life we are! We are tortured on the inside, mentally and emotionally, and as a result we torture ourselves relentlessly because we cannot *let go*. I know. I've been there.

I believe that we shall never walk in total peace and freedom until we are able to forgive from the heart. I believe that forgiveness is also a journey. There may well be many things for us to deal with, and to come to terms with, long before we can ever confront our fears and so forgive from the heart. I am aware that there may be some readers who, at this precise moment, will feel abused by what I am saying. And they may well want to scream: **'NO'**, tear this book up and throw it on the back of the fire, just as I wanted to do when I came to one particular passage in Tori Dante's book *Our Little Secret*. But I implore you to stay with me. First of all to set the scene, I must quote the review of Tori's book by Rob Parsons:

CHAPTER SEVENTEEN

"This book is shocking; there is simply no other word for it and all the more so because of the restrained way in which Tori Dante deals with the systematic abuse suffered at the hands of her own father. It must have cost her dearly to write it; we dare not ignore it". (Rob Parsons' review of *Our Little Secret* by Tori Dante).

In her book Tori Dante talks of visiting Maranatha Community, with a friend, for a session of what she calls 'life' prayer'. She writes:
"I wasn't sure what to expect and felt slightly apprehensive, but also very positive about what might happen after this time of prayer. I was asked to thank God for my creation, then to thank him for my ancestors and my bloodline... I was asked to give thanks for my parents. This was hard; at this stage I felt alone, I felt deserted by my mother. It took me a long time to give thanks for them. I cried a lot. At first I just couldn't get the words out, there was so much pain inside. I could feel my stomach in knots. Why should I thank God for them anyway? But when I did, I felt relief. It was important that I didn't just pretend to give thanks for them; I had to want to do it and then mean it. The next thing was to thank the Lord for my life. This too was hard. I started to cry again and got angry. Why should I thank him for my life? All I could think about was the pain." (*Our Little Secret* pages 178 & 179).

This was the point where I wanted to scream: **"NO!"** and throw her book away. In fact, I did actually toss it on the bed and broke down in tears. I knew at that point, I could not have endured such a session as that. This was an unbelievably painful moment, and I am crying now, profusely, as I write. I had, as you know, endured the session with the Lord in the vision of the mantles. With His help and grace I came to the place where I could forgive from the heart. Yet it was several years later, before I was able to thank God for everyone who had played a part in my life, for either good or for bad. The fact is we are all different. It took almost five years to come to that wonderful place where I could recognise and accept in all truth and honesty the words of Joseph: "But as for you, you meant it for evil against me; but God meant it for good" (Genesis 50:20).

I have written in my acknowledgements these words, and I quote:

"I acknowledge all who played a part in my journey, both for good and for bad. To all who caused me harm, wittingly or unwittingly, there is no animosity on my part. Without their part the story would not be complete and I would not be the person I am today."

Do you think I wrote those words for sentiment? "Oh bless him! That is nice." Do you think I wrote it for effect or maybe for a pat on the back? Certainly not! It took a great deal of courage, through much pain and many tears to pen those words and mean it from the heart. This is no game that we are playing. It is very real and deadly serious; our status in eternity could very well depend on the resolution of our resentments.

My dear friends, one way or another, we have to get beyond our 'victim mentality' and believe God. Let's be real here. Today is Tuesday the 5th of October 2010 and in two weeks to this very day I shall be sixty years old. I don't have time to pussyfoot around and wallow in self-pity or spend my time in blaming someone else and in finding somebody who will 'stroke' my wounds and 'kiss' them better.

I say, "Get over it and get a life!" In other words, begin changing your thinking and ask God to help you to face your grudges and bitterness. This is what I mean when I say "get over it" — this **will** undoubtedly be difficult and it will be a journey. But if we don't come to terms with these issues, we are in danger of carrying our bitter and twisted heart to the grave. Believe me, I have wasted the majority of my lifetime

CHAPTER SEVENTEEN

bearing grudges and walking in unforgiveness. It is only now that I feel I am getting my life back. This is what I mean by saying "get a life".

Please understand this. The things that drive us to bear a grudge, to be bitter about, or cause us to walk in unforgiveness are like splinters; they hurt going in and they will hurt coming out! It was difficult coming to terms with my own grudges and bitterness. It was unbelievably painful to face the unforgiveness of my own heart, but the result of meeting them head-on amazed me. When I genuinely forgave from the heart, I was filled with an indescribable joy. In a very short space of time the depth of healing generated from my forgiving, permeated the whole of my being. The freedom from the bitterness, the pain, the hurt, the sorrow, and the grief I'd carried as a result of my own unforgiveness was truly sublime.

- **Triggers.**

Triggers can be people, situations, places, events, smells, tastes, noises and sounds or anything that will 'trigger' a subconscious memory or reaction fuelling an addiction. If for instance the trigger is a person, that person doesn't have to say anything, do anything or offer anything; they simply have to **be**. That was a powerful revelation to me, which seemed to carry with it chilling undertones or connotations. I recall the following incident.

I was gazing through the window of my lounge (many years ago) and quite by chance, the fellow who had abused me as a teenager walked by. Terror struck my heart even though he hadn't seen me. There was a brick wall between us and I was no longer on his agenda, and yet terror had gripped my heart! After he had passed by, a drinking binge ensued. I had allowed that man to become a trigger to fuel my habit.

This incident came to mind during the vision of the mantles, although I didn't make it known when I shared that vision. As the reality and implications of this trigger dawned upon me, I confessed them before God, taking ownership of the part I had played in **allowing** that man to become a trigger. I took responsibility for my own actions and began to cease blaming him. I repented before God and I was genuinely sorry for my drinking and the part I had played in the apportioning of blame and the subsequent bearing of a grudge. Finally I forgave.

That fellow had in fact done nothing wrong at that point; he'd merely walked by my lounge window. My reactions of anger, hatred and the drinking binges were of my **own** making and no one else's. I had to forgive for my own therapy and for my own emotional well-being. I was **not** going to play the **victim** any more. By forgiving him from the heart, I was actually *letting go* of the rubbish I'd carried around for so many years. This process will undoubtedly have to be repeated many times over in order to break the cycle. Nevertheless, repeat it we must. We dare not allow triggers to rule us, for this will serve no other purpose than to keep us trapped.

This was but one of several triggers that had kept me trapped in alcoholism. Slowly, one by one, they surfaced. When the Lord made something known to me, I turned my face towards Him in prayer and 'waited' with more determination — waiting day by day, until He showed me how to deal with it. I'd try not to be hasty at all. To panic, I sensed, would have been folly. So I attempted to follow my prescribed route quietly. As the Psalmist says: "Commune with God in your heart and be still". (Psalm 4:4, AV). Unresolved triggers hinder recovery and the victory we believe to be ours becomes unsustainable. In my opinion, one of the main reasons why there may not be instant deliverance from addictions or dependency when prayed for, is simply 'unresolved triggers'.

CHAPTER SEVENTEEN

- **Fear**

    The Twelve Steps manual says:
    "Fear is often our first response to anything new. We meet change with fear because we feel threatened by so many things. Fear creates a physical response that begins with the release of adrenaline and ends up with the whole body on alert. This alerted state often leads to persistent and unwanted tension and can develop into stress related illness." (*The Twelve Steps* page 79).

    My mental, emotional and physical problems were stress related and, if thought through carefully, they can be traced back to fear. Throughout this treatise I have been quite open and honest about my fears and I've tried to show how I faced them and how God helped me to overcome them. Fear paralyses and prevents us from acting appropriately. "Fear involves torment" (1 John 4:18). Fear must be addressed.

    "Fear is an underlying cause of many forms of spiritual disease. It is the first response we feel when we aren't in control of a situation. A wide range of mental and physical ills are frequently the direct result of this unwholesome emotion. Fear often prevents us from seeing options to effectively resolve the issue causing the fear. Learning to acknowledge fear in a healthy way is an important part of our recovery process." (*The Twelve Steps* page 82.)

    When a situation appeared out of my control I would 'fear'. My fear would cause tension and stress and the subsequent panic attacks would culminate in outbursts of anger and fits of rage followed by drinking binges, as I have described elsewhere. I was trapped in a vicious circle. Both my repressed anger and inappropriately expressed anger triggered resentment, depression, anxiety, self-pity, jealousy and stress. The result was imprisonment in a fundamentally unwholesome cycle. Fear of failure, fear of criticism, fear of rejection, fear of insecurity and fear of identity loss, caused me to overreact to change. Just a simple change, like an item of my clothing being moved out of what I thought was its rightful place, was enough to send me over the top. I became intolerant, overly judgemental and expressed very strong opinions. This was my 'torment' (1 John 4:18), and this was fear in the extreme. It's a small wonder that I became ill and displayed symptoms of Chronic Fatigue Syndrome.

The Twelve Steps manual says:
"Many of us have difficulty expressing our feelings or even realizing we have them. We harbour deep emotional pain and a sense of guilt and shame. As children, our feelings were met with disapproval, anger, and rejection. For survival purposes, we learned to hide our feelings or repress them entirely. As adults, we are not in touch with our feelings.... Distorted and repressed feelings cause resentment, anger, and depression, which often lead to physical illness." (*The Twelve Steps* page 89.)

If I was going to break my addictions I surely had to face my fears. Fear is destructive. It is a major root of any addiction, dependency or bondage. It may be difficult to detect but it will be there, lying masked beneath inappropriate responses or reactions. Your fears, of course, will be different from mine; nevertheless, you will have to face them at some point in order to walk free.

- **Abuse.**

    There are many areas of abuse, but I have elected to focus upon just four. They are: physical abuse, verbal abuse, emotional abuse and sexual abuse.

I know very little about physical abuse. My own experience was nothing more than a little bullying at school. Nevertheless, it did have an effect upon me and has caused me to respond in an adverse fashion to domination, intimidation and manipul-

CHAPTER SEVENTEEN

ation — three things I loathe to this very day.

There are very many people who have suffered terrible physical abuse. As children some have endured horrendous bullying at school. At home, others have been tortured, having been beaten, burnt and scalded or locked away in closets. These people bear the scars, physically, mentally and emotionally and my heart genuinely goes out to them. Many, as a result, have contemplated suicide whilst some, tragically, have followed through and taken their own lives. Abuse is evil, destructive and deadly.

Throughout my time at school and nearly all of my working life I have been verbally and emotionally abused. These abuses were major factors contributing to my breakdown. They were soul-destroying and devastating to me. Sadly, I behaved the **victim** and allowed the abuse to fuel my addictions. I am not apportioning blame here. It was my own response to the abuse where the fault lay. I became timid as a result and felt inferior, but conversely, I had violent outbursts and fits of rage (as already pointed out). Tragically, my verbal outbursts and fits of rage were vented on those I loved and on those who were weaker than me (usually Maureen, my wife) and not the abusers. My physical acts of violence were vented on **things** rather than on people. I would throw things around and kick things up in the air. Thankfully, I never struck Maureen but I did frighten her.

As a child my mind shut down and had blotted out the horror and the memory of my own, repeated, sexual abuse. Blotting out various aspects of abuse appears to be quite common with abuse victims. Again I quote Tori Dante:
"It's strange, thinking back , but I blocked out so much of the pain and degradation of my own experience that, superficially, I hardly feel any pain for myself." (*Our Little Secret*, page 20.)
This was my subconscious coping mechanism in action. My

memory of childhood abuse returned in stages. For me it began to return during the vision of the 'mantles' (late 2004). A couple of months later, I was due to go on a Healing Weekend at Ellel Grange, Ellel, Lancashire, LA2 0HN, England. E-mail: 'info@grange.ellel.org.uk'. I went there with the firm intention of meeting this issue of childhood sexual abuse head-on. My friend Steve Buck accompanied me as my 'carer'. More of my childhood memory returned in the counselling room. It was a very difficult experience and I cried rivers of tears. The truth is, it is never easy, nor is it going to be. We are only kidding ourselves if we think it is. But, God knows what He is doing. We have to trust God in that respect, by trusting that He is guiding the counsellor.

That took place in the early spring of 2005. But it was much later, in the spring of 2010 while engaged in the writing of this narrative, that even more of my memory returned. I honestly do not think I could have handled it if the memory had returned all at once. Tori Dante, speaking of her healing, says: "If God had healed me in an instant I would not have known who I was! I would have had an identity crisis." (*Our Little Secret*, page 183.)

Whether we are thinking about healing or memory, I thank God that He knows what He is doing and what we can take; and He works either slowly or quickly for our benefit.

Painfully, I relived the abuse on that weekend retreat in the counselling room... but I forgave... I repented of my anger... bitterness... and hatred toward my abuser. I also 'forgave' myself. That act was important — not because the abuse was my fault, but because of a deep-down (subconscious) feeling that I **was** to blame in some way. One could very easily feel that the reason for the abuse was some underlying personal defect. One could also feel dirty or unclean because of that abuse. These were the reasons why I forgave myself. I quote

CHAPTER SEVENTEEN

Tori Dante once more:
"I think some people have a problem forgiving themselves. But for me, if God was willing to forgive me for all the wrong things I had done, then I am so grateful. And if he can forgive me, and he's God, then surely I must move on and forgive myself." (*Our Little Secret*, page 118.)

I had been messed up in my mind long enough; I didn't want to continue being tainted for the rest of my life. If freedom was within reach then I wanted to grasp it with both hands. To forgive my abuser certainly wasn't easy; it was painful and it hurt a lot, but the healing afterwards was so... so sweet. Words cannot describe what it was like. The best I can come up with is that it was like a load of excrement, full of worms and smothered in flies and maggots being lifted off my back!!

Before you wonder where all that came from, allow me to explain. Just prior to my encounter with God at Ellel Grange, I again had a visionary dream. I was bowed low with a mucky, heavy pack on my back (as described) and the Lord Jesus came and lifted it off me. My back was raw and torn with open wounds and sores but gradually it healed. The joy was indescribable. However, I came away from Ellel Grange with a feeling as if I'd undergone major surgery.

18

Putting Things into Perspective

> As children bring their broken toys
> With tears for us to mend,
> I brought my broken dreams to God
> Because He was my friend.
> But then, instead of leaving Him
> In peace to work alone,
> I hung around and tried to help
> With ways that were my own.
> At last, I snatched them back and cried,
> 'How can You be so slow?'
> 'My child,' He said,
> 'What could I do? You never did let go.'
>
> *Author unknown.* (Taken from *The Twelve Steps*.)

We are all different and everyone's journey is different; there is no one set pattern for deliverance. Certain things apply and are constants, yes, but the journey that God takes us on is 'tailor-made' for each of us and it takes time. "Why so long?" and "Why so difficult?" you may well ask. I've asked myself those questions many times over. It is my view that there are many things in our lives that prevent us from breaking our addictions, and must first be dealt with, such as the 'roots' I've mentioned in the previous chapter. These things often take time

CHAPTER EIGHTEEN

to come to light. They hinder recovery, cause repetitive bad behaviour and prevent us from entering into freedom. To face these issues and to deal with them is, in my opinion, crucial to recovery. In *The Twelve Steps* we are encouraged in Step Four to prepare a personal inventory:
"Being totally honest in preparing our inventory is vital to the self discovery that forms the foundation of our recovery. It allows us to remove obstacles that have prevented us from knowing ourselves and truthfully acknowledging our deepest feelings about life." (*The Twelve Steps* page 70.)

Honesty, in my opinion, is an absolute necessity. We must also accept what we discover about ourselves, whether good or bad. Again I quote from *The Twelve Steps* manual:
"This acceptance will free us to discover survival behaviours that began in childhood. In the context of our turbulent early years, these behaviours were lifesaving. However, their continuation into our adulthood renders us dysfunctional." (page 70.)

Below I examine briefly a further matter of importance in our quest for freedom. I explore several pitfalls and points to avoid, and I also ponder the visions and visitations. I raise such questions as: Why did He come to me? Does it make me any more spiritual than others for having seen the Lord? Finally, I consider the significance of the Lord's message and His manner of dealing with me, in order to give a fair appraisal of what had taken place.

The Renewal of the Mind: There must be a conscious and deliberate effort on our part to change our thinking. We can set in motion a series of simple things to bring about such a change in thought. Joyce Meyer in her book *Battlefield of the Mind* speaks from her own experience:
"Although I was a Christian, I was having trouble because I had

not learned to control my thoughts. I thought about things that kept my mind busy but were not productive in a positive way. *I needed to change my thinking!* One thing the Lord told me when He began to teach me about the battlefield of the mind became a major turning point for me. He said, 'Think about what you're thinking about.' As I began to do so, it was not long before I began to see why I was having so much trouble in my life. *My mind was a mess!* I was thinking all the wrong things. I went to church, and had done so for years, but I never actually thought about what I heard. It went in one ear and out the other, so to speak. I read some Scriptures in the Bible every day, but never thought about what I was reading. I was not *attending* to the Word. I was not giving thought and study to what I was hearing. Therefore, no virtue or knowledge was coming back to me." (Joyce Meyer, *Battlefield of the Mind*, page 66.)

In other words, I had to think about what I was thinking and meditate on the Scriptures (the Bible). In addition, I slowed myself right down inside and began to wait on God in prayer (as outlined throughout this narrative). Constantly I *let go*. I let go of all sorts of stuff in my mind that kept me trapped and released it to God. To let go and to release my inward hold, followed by a change of mind (repentance) was absolutely crucial in my breaking free process. Then I set myself to **believe** and to **obey** the Word (the Scriptures).

To put all that together, you have what I believe the Bible calls the 'renewing of the mind'. "And do not be conformed to this world, but be transformed by the renewing of your mind, that you may prove what is that good and acceptable and perfect will of God" (Romans 12:2). Such a practice is imperative to those with dependency problems and those who have to deal with emotional issues. The process of renewing the mind takes time and where there is no instant deliverance,

CHAPTER EIGHTEEN

as in my case, that process can be an arduous and time-consuming journey.

Holding back: I have mentioned elsewhere in this narrative that changes were taking place rather quickly, so quickly in fact I was concerned that I wouldn't be able to keep up. My fear, unbeknown to me, called a halt and put a block on God's work. Being fearful of the future and doubting my own ability to go forward with God held me back. I'm shaking my head in disbelief as I write. How could I possibly have been so foolish? As if **my** ability had anything to do with it! For in so doing, I only hindered God's process of deeper growth and healing. The result of holding back is that one has to learn the 'lesson' all over again (whatever that lesson is). For some reason, no one ever seems to pick up where they leave off and it always seems much harder the second time around. I have held back on several occasions. I pray to God that it doesn't become a habit; I don't want to hold back the next time.

It is not easy throwing caution to the wind in formerly uncharted waters, for the alcoholic or addict has no idea what freedom is like. Until, of course, he or she gets there, and tastes it for themselves. And when they do, it often tastes different from what was expected. It is a journey of faith and often we learn by trial and error, success and failure, but to hold back will serve no other purpose than to delay or hinder God's work.

Unbelief: Another reason why we may delay or hinder God's process of victory is simply unbelief — our failure to believe what God reveals to us. God's message may come to us via revelation or an inner 'voice' (impression or impulse) or through the reading of the Scriptures. It may come through another person, in private conversation, in the counselling room, in group therapy, or in a sermon. Failure to believe God's message and to act upon it can be a great hindrance to God's work in our lives.

Holding back and unbelief are just two reasons, of our own making, why it can take so long to step into the victory of Christ.

What about the visitations? There are several things I'd like to say and questions I'd like to attempt to answer regarding the visitations in order to put things into perspective.

Why did He come to me? That is one question I cannot fully answer, but it is very humbling that He did. I was and still am the weakest of the weak. The Lord has kept His word and has not fully healed my mind. Every day I have to set in motion what He taught me through the revelatory visions. I cannot escape from that. If I don't do it, my mind will wander and begin to go out of control. I have no other means at my disposal, of staying close to God, other than through the prayer of quiet, which is a moment-by-moment thing. If I don't stay close, very soon I will begin to fall away. I know because it has happened to me so many times.

I was and still am the lowest of the low. I fell into sin as a Christian, wilfully and with my eyes open. I was in the church! I was in church leadership! I had gifting and was held in high regard! Yet I had a prodigal heart! If we fall into gross sin as a Christian, wilfully and with our eyes open, **there will be no easy way back.** You cannot play around with God. But my story does serve to declare that **there is** indeed a way back and there is a way of intimacy.

This still doesn't answer the question, why He came and why He came so often. I have no real answer other than **Outrageous Grace.** Why 'outrageous'? Well, it is an outrage, scandalous in fact; that the sow that was washed and "had gone back to wallowing in the mire" (2 Peter 2:22), should find a way back! It is 'outrageous' that the Son of the Almighty should come to a 'dog who had returned to his own vomit' (2 Peter 2:22), and **sit** down with him in that **vomit!** But that's

CHAPTER EIGHTEEN

exactly what He did and if we are honest, He's done the very same thing with all of us.

It was an 'outrage' to the Pharisee (Luke 7:36-50) when the woman came to Jesus with the alabaster flask of perfume and anointed Him with its contents, washed His feet with her tears and dried them with her hair. "This man, if he were a prophet, would know who and what manner of woman this is who is touching him, for she is a sinner." (Luke 7:39)

It was likewise an 'outrage' to the older brother, when the prodigal son returned and the father put a ring on his finger, gave him the finest robe, put sandals upon his feet and killed the fattened calf for a celebration. (Luke 15:11-32)

My acceptance of the things I have just shared has been wonderfully freeing and liberating. Far from feeling rejected and inferior, I am now content and at peace with who I am. I have no words to say; my heart is stripped bare; only my **tears** can now suffice, which now spring from a **joy** that is inexpressible and full of **Glory**.

Does it make you any better or more spiritual for having seen the Lord? Certainly **not!** Those who have never seen a vision, never seen angels or never seen the Lord, are they any less spiritual? Certainly **not!** The Christian experience is all about Faith and not about Sight. "For we walk by faith, not by sight." (2 Corinthians 5:7). But examine also, if you will, the words of Jesus to Thomas. "Thomas, because you have seen me, you have believed. **Blessed** are those who have not seen and yet have believed." (John 20:29) Better, in my opinion, is a person who has never had a vision, never seen an angel or never seen the Lord and yet is able to believe, trust in God and walk with Him through all of life's hardships, honouring Him in all they say and do. Nothing is greater than that. The key issue is **faith**.

The person, on the other hand, who has seen such things

carries a very great burden of responsibility. They must not think too highly of themselves. Everything they share must be shared for the glory of God. Some things they have seen must not be shared under any circumstances. They must learn how to listen for God or else they will greatly dishonour their Lord.

It is human nature to think that one is in some way special. But we must get rid of such notions; they must die the death. I wanted to shout and tell the world, but God wouldn't let me. If, for whatever reason, Christ should choose to visit us, ultimately it will **not** be about us; it will be all about Him.

The three most important things I've discovered about any visitation are these: Firstly, the message He brings; secondly, what He reveals to us of Himself; thirdly, what we do with the message He brings.

The message He brings: The Apostle Paul encountered the resurrected Christ on the road to Damascus and was stunned by His message, "Saul, Saul, why are you persecuting me?" (Acts 9:4). Those words must have rocked His world.

When the Lord Jesus visited me the first time, I too was stunned by His appearing; it terrified me and shook me to the very core. The message to me was in His actions; He came and embraced me. That action spoke volumes to my heart. I didn't think that God could love me, because of my wilful prodigal heart, nor did I consider myself to be lovable either. Inside, I felt as though I was a reject and sitting on a muck tip. He came where I was and embraced me. That action was a powerful message to my soul.

What He reveals to us of Himself: Paul said to Jesus: " 'Who are you Lord?' Then the Lord said, 'I am Jesus, whom you are persecuting'." (Acts 9:5). Just exactly what was revealed to Paul of the person of Christ contained in those words, 'I am Jesus, whom you are persecuting', one can only imagine. But what he saw of Jesus changed his life.

CHAPTER EIGHTEEN

The side of His person that He revealed to me was 'GRACE', and that was overwhelming. It is my belief that in any visitation, He always comes to us 'veiled' in some way. He only reveals to us what He wants us to see or know. When He came to me, I would have liked to have seen His POWER — His power to heal, to transform and to deliver. But that side I didn't see. What He showed me instead was but a **kiss** of love and grace. The part of His person He reveals to us is pertinent to the message He brings. "It's hard for you to kick against the goads," He said to Paul. With my encounter, I cried so much that I could hardly catch my breath and my ribs ached as though I'd taken a good beating; but **He wept with me!** Having been touched by the breath of eternity, I am convinced that if He were to reveal Himself, as He really is in His entirety, then we would die. We would not be able to contain Him; of that I have no doubt whatsoever.

What we do with the message He brings: With the first two issues, we have no control or influence at all; it is entirely up to Him, He chooses and does according to His will and what He sees fit. What we do with the message He brings is up to us. This is the weight of responsibility that we carry. For this reason the heart must slow down, be still, turn to the Lord and listen.

When the Lord appeared to Saul of Tarsus on the road to Damascus, He said to him: "Arise and go into the city, and you will be told what you must do." (Acts 9:6). Obedience to the message is crucial. Paul went into the city and waited in prayer. Then the prophetic message came through a man named Ananias. (Acts 9:10–19) Paul sought to obey that message. Solomon on the other hand did not. It is with a sad heart that I have to report that Solomon's love of foreign women led him astray. The Scripture says: "... his heart was not loyal to the Lord his God, as was the heart of his father David". (1 Kings

11:4). "So the Lord became angry with Solomon, because his heart had turned from the Lord God of Israel, who had appeared to him twice." (1 Kings 11:9). What a tragedy! The Lord had appeared to Solomon on two occasions but he hadn't fully obeyed the message.

What we do with the message God brings to us is of the utmost importance. His message to me was in His embrace, meaning: — 'stay close to me'. His message was also in His tears as He wept with me, meaning: — 'be sensitive to the needs of others'. I can only hope and trust that I'll be able to fulfil His message and embrace others with the love with which Christ embraced me.

The way forward: I count myself highly honoured to have been afforded the privilege of finding God in prayer. However, at no stage did I think... 'I know, I'll try praying my way out of this mess!' because prayer in the normal fashion didn't appear to be working for me. Although I was a Christian, I was a lost soul. Not in the sense that I was damned and had lost my Salvation; but I was wandering aimlessly and could not find my way.

My journey into freedom was not instigated by me; it was all instigated by God. If Jesus had not come to me and told me what to do, I dread to think where I would be now. At the very least I'd still be 'feeding pigs', wallowing around in the mire and longing to be 'fed the husks' but getting no sustenance (couching it in 'Prodigal Son' terms, Luke 15:11-32). I might even have been dead by now, given the way I was going and the state of my mind, for I was indeed near to pressing the self-destruct button on many occasions.

JESUS SET ME FREE... Consequently, I felt honour bound to tell my story and share with you what God has done for me. Now, for me the journey into freedom really begins. Who knows where it will take me?

Bibliography

Amplified Bible, The – Zondervan, Grand Rapids, Michigan 49530 U.S.A. 1987

Dante, Tori – *Our Little Secret*, Hodder & Stoughton, London, 2001

Day, Joff – *Forgive, Release and be Free*, Sovereign World Ltd, PO Box 777 Tonbridge Kent TN11 0ZS 2004

Guyon, Jeanne – *Experiencing the Depths of Jesus Christ*, SeedSowers Christian Books Publishing House, PO Box 3317 Jacksonville, FL 32206

Hacking, W – *A Life Ablaze with the Power of God*, Harrison House, Tulsa, Oklahoma 1995

Meyer, Joyce – *Battlefield of the Mind*, Warner Faith, New York, Boston, Nashville 1995

Molinos, Michael – *The Spiritual Guide*, SeedSowers Christian Books Publishing House, PO Box 3317 Jacksonville, FL 32206

Oxford Quick Reference Dictionary, The – Oxford University Press, New York 1996

Spirit-Filled Life Bible: New King James Version –.Jack Hayford (ed.), Thomas Nelson, Inc. Nashville, 1991

The Twelve Steps – A Spiritual Journey; A Working Guide for Healing – R. P. I. Publishing, Inc. San Diego 1994

Books for Further Reading

If Amy Carmichael; SPCK Holy Trinity Church, Marylebone Road, London NW1 4DU

Mystical Paths to God: Three Journeys: Brother Lawrence's *The Practice of the Presence of God*, St. Teresa of Avila's *Interior Castle*, St. John of the Cross's *Dark Night of the Soul* Wilder Publications, LLC. PO Box3005 Radford VA 24143

Practicing His Presence Brother Lawrence & Frank Laubach, SeedSowers Christian Books Publishing House PO Box 3317 Jacksonville, FL 32206
Praying Hyde Captain E.G. Carre, Bridge Publishing, Monmouth, Gwent, UK
Rees Howells, Intercessor Norman Grubb, Lutterworth Press www.lutterworth.com
Spiritual Torrents Jeanne Guyon, SeedSowers PO Box 285 Sargent, GA 30275
The Normal Christian Life Watchman Nee, Kingsway Publications, Eastbourne, UK.

If you have been touched by any of the issues raised in this book and would like to speak to Rob in depth, or if you would like him to speak at your church or group meeting, you may contact him by email:
rob-giles2011@hotmail.co.uk

Э/Р